TOSEL
교재 Series

교재별 연계

TOSEL LEVEL	Age	Vocabulary Frequency	Readability Score	교과 과정 연계	Grammar	VOCA	Reading	Listening
Cocoon	K5-K7	500	0-1	Who is he? (국어 1단원 1-1)	There is · There are	150	Picking Pumpkins (Phonics Story)	Phonics
Pre-Starter	P1-P2	700	1-2	How old are you? (통합교과 1-1)	be + adjective	300	Me & My Family (Reading series Ch.1)	묘사하기
Starter	P3-P4	1000-2000	1-2	Spring, Summer, Fall, Winter (통합교과 3-1)	Simple Present	800	Ask More Questions (Reading Series Ch.1)	날씨/시간 표현
Basic	P5-P6	3000-4000	3-4	Show and Tell (사회 5-1)	Superlative	1700	Culture (Reading Series Ch.3)	상대방 의견 묻고 답하기
Junior	M1-M2	5000-6000	5-6	중 1, 2 과학, 기술가정	to-infinitive	4000	Humans and Animals (Reading Series Ch.1)	정보 묻고 답하기
High Junior	H1-H3	5000-6000	5-6	고등학교 - 체육	2nd Conditional	7000	Health (Reading Series Ch.1)	사건 묘사하기

■ TOSEL의 세분화된 레벨은 각 연령에 맞는 어휘와 읽기 지능 및 교과 과정과의 연계가
가능하도록 설계된 교재들로 효과적인 학습 커리큘럼을 제공합니다.

■ TOSEL의 커리큘럼에 따른 학습은
정확한 레벨링 → 레벨에 적합한 학습 → 영어 능력 인증 시험 TOSEL에서의 공신력 있는 평가를 통해
진단 → 학습 → 평가의 선순환 구조를 실현합니다.

About TOSEL®

TOSEL은 각급 학교 교과과정과 연령별 인지단계를 고려하여 단계별 난이도와 문항으로
영어 숙달 정도를 측정하는 영어 사용자 중심의 맞춤식 영어능력인증 시험제도입니다.
평가유형에 따른 개인별 장점과 단점을 파악하고, 개인별 영어학습 방향을 제시하는 성적분석자료를 제공하여
영어능력 종합검진 서비스를 제공함으로써 영어 사용자인 소비자와
영어능력 평가를 토대로 영어교육을 담당하는 교사 및 기관 인사관리자인 공급자를
모두 만족시키는 영어능력인증 평가입니다.

TOSEL은 인지적-학문적 언어 사용의 유창성 (Cognitive-Academic Language Proficiency, CALP)과
기본적-개인적 의사소통능력 (Basic Interpersonal Communication Skill, BICS)을
엄밀히 구분하여 수험자의 언어능력을 가장 친밀하게 평가하는 시험입니다.

대상	목적	용도
유아, 초, 중, 고등학생, 대학생 및 직장인 등 성인	한국인의 영어구사능력 증진과 비영어권 국가의 영어 사용자의 영어구사능력 증진	실질적인 영어구사능력 평가 + 입학전형 및 인재선발 등에 활용 및 직무역량별 인재 배치

연혁

2002.02	국제토셀위원회 창설 (수능출제위원역임 전국대학 영어전공교수진 중심)
2004.09	TOSEL 고려대학교 국제어학원 공동인증시험 실시
2006.04	EBS 한국교육방송공사 주관기관 참여
2006.05	민족사관고등학교 입학전형에 반영
2008.12	고려대학교 편입학시험 TOSEL 유형으로 대체
2009.01	서울시 공무원 근무평정에 TOSEL 점수 가산점 부여
2009.01	전국 대부분 외고, 자사고 입학전형에 TOSEL 반영 (한영외국어고등학교, 한일고등학교, 고양외국어고등학교, 과천외국어고등학교, 김포외국어고등학교, 명지외국어고등학교, 부산국제외국어고등학교, 부일외국어 고등학교, 성남외국어고등학교, 인천외국어고등학교, 전북외국어고등학교, 대전외국어고등학교, 청주외국어고등학교, 강원외국어고등학교, 전남외국어고등학교)
2009.12	청심국제중·고등학교 입학전형 TOSEL 반영
2009.12	한국외국어교육학회, 팬코리아영어교육학회, 한국음성학회, 한국응용언어학회 TOSEL 인증
2010.03	고려대학교, TOSEL 출제기관 및 공동 인증기관으로 참여
2010.07	경찰청 공무원 임용 TOSEL 성적 가산점 부여
2014.04	전국 200개 초등학교 단체 응시 실시
2017.03	중앙일보 주관기관 참여
2018.11	관공서, 대기업 등 100여 개 기관에서 TOSEL 반영
2019.06	미얀마 TOSEL 도입 발족식 베트남 TOSEL 도입 협약식
2019.11	2020학년도 고려대학교 편입학전형 반영
2020.04	국토교통부 국가자격시험 TOSEL 반영
2021.07	소방청 간부후보생 선발시험 TOSEL 반영

High Junior 2권

TOSEL® Level Chart TOSEL 단계표

COCOON
아이들이 접할 수 있는 공식 인증 시험의 첫 단계로써, 아이들의 부담을 줄이고 즐겁게 흥미를 유발할 수 있도록 컬러풀한 색상과 디자인으로 시험지를 구성하였습니다.

Pre-STARTER
친숙한 주제에 대한 단어, 짧은 대화, 짧은 문장을 사용한 기본적인 문장표현 능력을 측정합니다.

STARTER
흔히 접할 수 있는 주제와 상황과 관련된 주제에 대한 짧은 대화 및 짧은 문장을 이해하고 일상생활 대화에 참여하며 실질적인 영어 기초 의사소통 능력을 측정합니다.

BASIC
개인 정보와 일상 활동, 미래 계획, 과거의 경험에 대해 구어와 문어의 형태로 의사소통을 할 수 있는 능력을 측정합니다.

JUNIOR
일반적인 주제와 상황을 다루는 회화와 짧은 단락, 실용문, 짧은 연설 등을 이해하고 간단한 일상 대화에 참여하는 능력을 측정합니다.

HIGH JUNIOR
넓은 범위의 사회적, 학문적 주제에서 영어를 유창하고 정확하게, 효과적으로 사용할 수 있는 능력 및 중문과 복잡한 문장을 포함한 다양한 문장구조의 사용 능력을 측정합니다.

ADVANCED
대학 및 대학원에서 요구되는 영어능력과 취업 또는 직업근무환경에 필요한 실용영어 능력을 측정합니다.

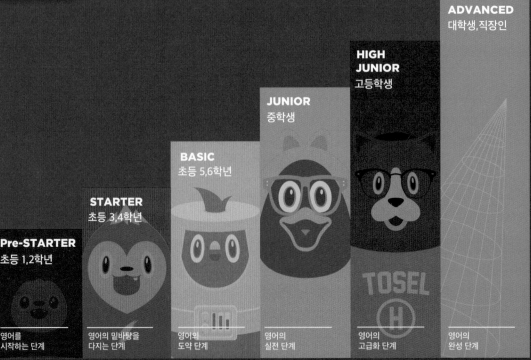

ADVANCED
대학생, 직장인

HIGH JUNIOR
고등학생

JUNIOR
중학생

BASIC
초등 5,6학년

STARTER
초등 3,4학년

Pre-STARTER
초등 1,2학년

COCOON
유치원생

영어의 첫 걸음 단계.

영어를 시작하는 단계.

영어의 밑바탕을 다지는 단계.

영어의 도약 단계.

영어의 실전 단계.

영어의 고급화 단계.

영어의 완성 단계.

TOSEL®
HIGH JUNIOR

 International TOSEL Committee

GRAMMAR 1

CONTENTS

About **TOSEL**®

What's TOSEL?

> **"Test of Skills in the English Language"**

TOSEL은 비영어권 국가의 영어 사용자를 대상으로 영어구사능력을 측정하여
그 결과를 공식 인증하는 영어능력인증 시험제도입니다.

영어 사용자 중심의 맞춤식 영어능력 인증 시험제도

맞춤식 평가

**획일적인 평가에서
세분화된 평가로의 전환**

TOSEL은 응시자의 연령별
인지단계에 따라 별도의 문항과 난이도를
적용하여 평가함으로써 평가의
목적과 용도에 적합한 평가 시스템을
구축하였습니다.

공정성과 신뢰성 확보

국제토셀위원회의 역할

TOSEL은 고려대학교가 출제 및 인증기관
으로 참여하였고 대학입학수학능력시험
출제위원 교수들이 중심이 된
국제토셀위원회가 주관하여
사회적 공정성과 신뢰성을 확보한
평가 제도입니다.

수입대체 효과

외화유출 차단 및 국위선양

TOSEL은 해외시험응시로 인한 외화의
유출을 막는 수입대체의 효과를 기대할 수
있습니다. TOSEL의 문항과 시험제도는
비영어권 국가에 수출하여 국위선양에
기여하고 있습니다.

Why TOSEL® ——— 왜 TOSEL인가

01 학교 시험 폐지

일선 학교에서 중간, 기말고사 폐지로 인해 객관적인 영어 평가 제도의 부재가 우려됩니다. 그러나 전국단위로 연간 4번 시행되는 TOSEL 평가시험을 통해 학생들은 정확한 역량과 체계적인 학습방향을 꾸준히 진단받을 수 있습니다.

02 연령별/단계별 대비로 영어학습 점검

TOSEL은 응시자의 연령별 인지단계 및 영어 학습 단계에 따라 총 7단계로 구성되었습니다. 각 단계에 알맞은 문항유형과 난이도를 적용해 모든 연령 및 학습 과정에 맞추어 가장 효율적으로 영어실력을 평가할 수 있도록 개발된 영어시험입니다.

03 학교내신성적 향상

TOSEL은 학년별 교과과정과 연계하여 학교에서 배우는 내용을 학습하고 평가할 수 있도록 문항 및 주제를 구성하여 내신영어 향상을 위한 최적의 솔루션을 제공합니다.

04 수능대비 직결

유아, 초, 중등시절 어렵지 않고 즐겁게 학습해 온 영어이지만, 수능시험준비를 위해 접하는 영어의 문항 및 유형 난이도에 주춤하게 됩니다. 이를 대비하기 위해 TOSEL은 유아부터 성인까지 점진적인 학습을 통해 수능대비를 자연적으로 해나갈 수 있습니다.

05 진학과 취업에 대비한 필수 스펙관리

개인별 '학업성취기록부' 발급을 통해 영어학업성취이력을 꾸준히 기록한 영어학습 포트폴리오를 제공하여 영어학습 이력을 관리할 수 있습니다.

06 자기소개서에 토셀 기재

개별적인 진로 적성 Report를 제공하여 진로를 파악하고 자기소개서 작성시 적극적으로 활용할 수 있는 객관적인 자료를 제공합니다.

07 영어학습 동기부여

시험실시 후 응시자 모두에게 수여되는 인증서는 영어학습에 대한 자신감과 성취감을 고취시키고 동기를 부여합니다.

08 AI 분석 영어학습 솔루션

국내외 15,000여 개 학교·학원 단체 응시인원 중 엄선한 100만 명 이상의 실제 TOSEL 성적 데이터를 기반으로 영어인증시험 제도 중 세계 최초로 인공지능이 분석한 개인별 AI 정밀 진단 성적표를 제공합니다. 최첨단 AI 정밀진단 성적표는 최적의 영어 학습 솔루션을 제시하여 영어 학습에 소요되는 시간과 노력을 획기적으로 절감해줍니다.

09 명예의 전당, 우수협력기관 지정

우수교육기관은 'TOSEL 우수 협력 기관'에 지정되고, 각 시/도별, 최고득점자를 명예의 전당에 등재합니다.

Evaluation —————— 평가

평가의 기본원칙

TOSEL은 PBT(Paper Based Test)를 통하여 간접평가와 직접평가를 모두 시행합니다.

> **TOSEL**은 언어의 네 가지 요소인 **읽기, 듣기, 말하기, 쓰기 영역을 모두 평가합니다.**

문자언어 음성언어

읽기능력 **+** 듣기능력

쓰기능력   말하기능력

↓

대한민국 대표 영어능력 인증 시험제도

TOSEL®

Reading 읽기	모든 레벨의 읽기 영역은 직접 평가 방식으로 측정합니다.
Listening 듣기	모든 레벨의 듣기 영역은 직접 평가 방식으로 측정합니다.
Writing 쓰기	모든 레벨의 쓰기 영역은 간접 평가 방식으로 측정합니다.
Speaking 말하기	모든 레벨의 말하기 영역은 간접 평가 방식으로 측정합니다.

> **TOSEL**은 연령별 인지단계를 고려하여 **아래와 같이 7단계로 나누어 평가합니다.**

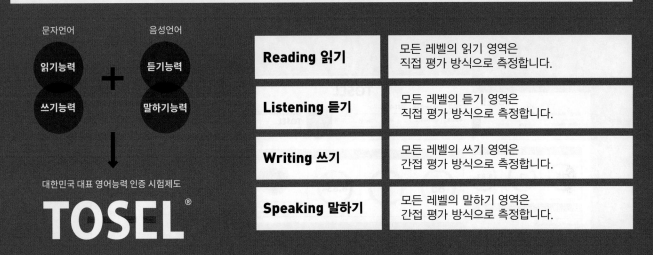

1 단계	TOSEL® COCOON	5~7세의 미취학 아동
2 단계	TOSEL® Pre-STARTER	초등학교 1~2학년
3 단계	TOSEL® STARTER	초등학교 3~4학년
4 단계	TOSEL® BASIC	초등학교 5~6학년
5 단계	TOSEL® JUNIOR	중학생
6 단계	TOSEL® HIGH JUNIOR	고등학생
7 단계	TOSEL® ADVANCED	대학생 및 성인

Grade Report

성적표 및 인증서

개인 AI 정밀진단 성적표

십 수년간 전국단위 정기시험으로 축적된 빅데이터를 교육공학적으로 분석 · 활용하여 산출한 개인별 성적자료

정확한 영어능력진단 / 섹션별 · 파트별 영어능력 및 균형 진단 / 명예의 전당 등재 여부 / 온라인 최적화된 개인별 상세
성적자료를 위한 QR코드 / 응시지역, 동일학년, 전국에서의 학생의 위치

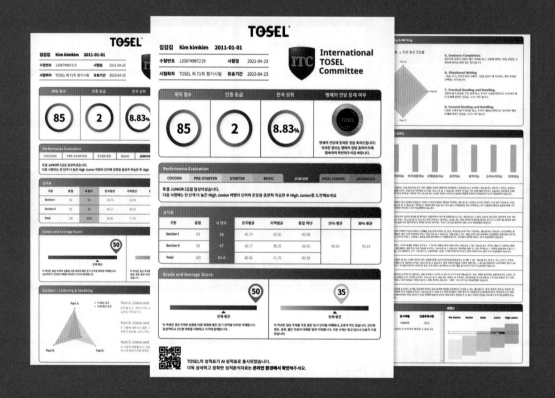

단체 및 기관 응시자 AI 통계 분석 자료

십 수년간 전국단위 정기시험으로 **축적된 빅데이터를
교육공학적으로 분석 · 활용**하여 산출한 응시자 통계 분석 자료

- 단체 내 레벨별 평균성적추이, LR평균 점수, 표준편차 파악
- 타 지역 내 다른 단체와의 점수 종합 비교 / 단체 내 레벨별
  학생분포 파악
- 동일 지역 내 다른 단체 레벨별 응시자의 평균 나이 비교
- 동일 지역 내 다른 단체 명예의 전당 등재 인원 수 비교
- 동일 지역 내 다른 단체 최고점자의 최고 점수 비교
- 동일 지역 내 다른 응시자들의 수 비교

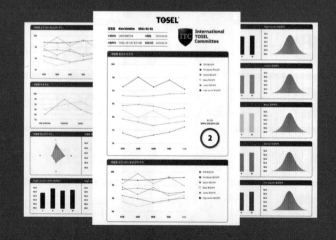

'토셀 명예의 전당' 등재

특별시, 광역시, 도 별 **1등 선발**
(7개시 9개도 **1등 선발**)

*홈페이지 로그인 - 시험결과 - 명예의 전당에서
 해당자 등재 증명서 출력 가능

'학업성취기록부'에 토셀 인증등급 기재

개인별 **'학업성취기록부'** 평생 발급
진학과 취업을 대비한 **필수 스펙관리**

인증서

대한민국 초,중,고등학생의 영어숙달능력 평가 결과 공식인증

고려대학교 인증획득 (2010. 03)   팬코리아영어교육학회 인증획득 (2009. 10)   한국응용언어학회 인증획득 (2009. 11)

한국외국어교육학회 인증획득 (2009. 12)   한국음성학회 인증획득 (2009. 12)

Grammar Series

TOSEL 시험을 기준으로 빈출 지표를 활용한 문법 선정 및 예문과 문제 구성

TOSEL 시험 활용

- 실제 TOSEL 시험에 출제된 빈출 문항을 기준으로 단계별 학습을 위한 문법 선정
- 실제 TOSEL 시험에 활용된 문장을 사용하여 예문과 문제를 구성
- 문법 학습 이외에 TOSEL 기출 문제 풀이를 통해서 TOSEL 및 실전 영어 시험 대비 학습

세분화된 레벨링

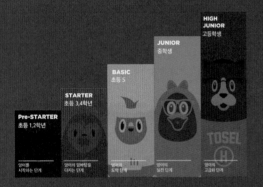

20년 간 대한민국 영어 평가 기관으로서

연간 4회 전국적으로 실시되는 정기시험에서

축적된 성적 데이터를 기반으로

정확하고 세분화된 레벨링을 통한

영어 학습 콘텐츠 개발

언어의 4대 영역 균형 학습 + 평가

1. TOSEL 평가: 학생의 영어 능력을 정확하게 평가

2. 결과 분석 및 진단: 시험 점수와 결과를 분석하여 학생의 강점, 취약점, 학습자 특성 등을 객관적으로 진단

3. 학습 방향 제시: 객관적 진단 데이터를 기반으로 학습자 특성에 맞는 학습 방향 제시 및 목표 설정

4. 학습: 제시된 방향과 목표에 따라 학생에게 적합한 문법 학습법 소개 및 영어의 체계와 구조 이해

5. 학습 목표 달성: 학습 후 다시 평가를 통해 목표 달성 여부 확인 및 성장을 위한 다음 학습 목표 설정

Grammar Series ——— Level

TOSEL의 Grammar Series는 레벨에 맞게 단계적으로
문법을 학습할 수 있도록 구성되어 있습니다.

Pre-Starter	Starter	Basic	Junior	High Junior

- ■ 그림을 활용하여 문법에 대한 이해도 향상
- ■ 다양한 활동을 통해 문법 반복 학습 유도
- ■ TOSEL 기출 문제 연습을 통한 실전 대비

- ■ TOSEL 기출의 빈도수를 활용한 문법 선정으로 효율적 학습
- ■ 실제 TOSEL 지문의 예문을 활용한 실용적 학습 제공
- ■ TOSEL 기출 문제 연습을 통한 실전 대비

최신 수능 출제
문법을 포함하여
수능 대비 가능

70분 학습 Guideline

01 💡 Unit Intro
2분

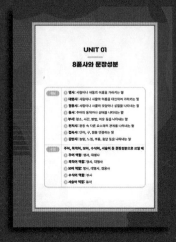
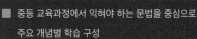

- ■ 중등 교육과정에서 익혀야 하는 문법을 중심으로 주요 개념별 학습 구성
- ■ 요약된 내용을 보고 단원의 개념에 대해 미리 생각해보기

02 📖 개념
15분

- ■ Unit Intro의 요약을 표로 구조화하여 세부적으로 학습하기 용이하게 구성

05 📖 Error Recognition
8분

- ■ 수능 유형의 실전 문제 학습을 통해 TOSEL 시험 뿐만 아니라 수능 영어 또한 대비 가능
- ■ 5개년 TOSEL 기출을 활용하여 더욱 생생한 문법

06 🧩 Unit Review
10분

- ■ 빈칸을 채우는 형태로 구성하여 수업 시간 후 복습에 용이하게 구성
- ■ 배운 문법을 활용하여 예시 문장을 직접 써보는 시간

03
⏱ Exercise

10분

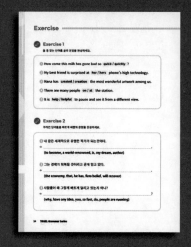

■ 다양한 Exercise 활동을 하며 혼동하기 쉬운
　　문법 학습

■ 문장 안에 문법적으로 알맞은 단어를 선택하거나
　　쓰는 활동을 하며 혼동하기 쉬운 문법 학습

04
✏ Sentence Completion

10분

■ Unit에서 배운 문법을 활용하여 문제 해결하기

■ 빈칸 채우기, 알맞은 표현 고르기 등 TOSEL 실전 문제 학습

■ 틀린 문제에 대해서는 해당 Unit에서 복습하도록 지도하기

07
TOSEL 실전문제

15분

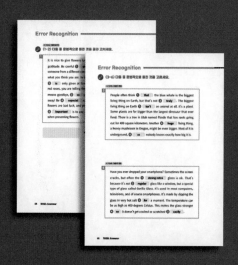

■ 실제 TOSEL 기출 문제를 통한 실전 대비 학습

■ 실제 시험 시간과 유사하게 풀이할 수 있도록 지도하기

■ 틀린 문제에 대해서는 해당 단원에서 복습하도록 지도하기

PreStarter/Starter/Basic Syllabus

PreStarter		Basic		2015 개정 초등 영어 언어형식
Chapter	Unit	Chapter	Unit	
I. 명사: 명사는 이름이야	1 셀 수 있는 명사	I. 명사	1 셀 수 있는 명사 앞에 붙는 관사 the/a/an	A boy/The **boy**/The (two) boys ran in the park. **The** store is closed.
	2 셀 수 있는 명사 앞에 붙는 관사 a/an		2 셀 수 없는 명사를 측정하는 단위	**Water** is very important for life. **Kate** is from **London**.
	3 셀 수 없는 명사		3 규칙 복수명사	The **two boys** ran in the park.
	4 명사의 복수형		4 불규칙 복수명사	
II. 대명사: 명사를 대신하는 대명사	1 주격 대명사	II. 대명사	1 단수대명사의 격	**She** is a teacher, and **he**'s a scientist. I like **your** glasses. What about **mine**?
	2 소유격 대명사		2 복수대명사의 격	**They**'re really delicious. **We** are very glad to hear from him.
	3 목적격 대명사		3 1, 2인칭 대명사의 활용	I like math, but Susan doesn't like **it**. He will help **you**.
	4 지시대명사		4 3인칭 대명사의 활용	Which do you like better, **this** or **that**? **These** are apples, and **those** are tomatoes. **That** dog is smart. **These/Those** books are really large.
III. 형용사: 명사&대명사를 꾸미는 형용사	1 형용사의 명사수식	III. 동사	1 동사의 기본시제	He **walks** to school every day. We **played** soccer yesterday. She **is going to** visit her grandparents next week. He **is sleeping** now. I **will visit** America next year.
	2 형용사의 대명사수식		2 동사의 불규칙 과거형	
	3 숫자와 시간		3 헷갈리기 쉬운 동사	It's **half past four**. **What time** is it?
				I **don't** like snakes. We **didn't** enjoy the movie very much.
	4 지시형용사		4 조동사	She **can** play the violin. Tom **won't** be at the meeting tomorrow. I **will** visit America next year. You **may** leave now.

Junior Syllabus

Junior		2015 개정 중등 영어 언어형식
Chapter	**Unit**	
I. 8품사 (1)	1 명사	She lived in the **woods** when she was kid. Thank you for your **kindness**.
	2 대명사	I have **three books**. **One** is mine. **The others** are yours. **The chocolate cookie** is sweet. I'm going to have **another one**.
	3 형용사	Something **strange** happened last night.
	4 감탄사	**How** beautiful she is! **What** a player!
II 8품사 (2)	1 동사	**Mathematics** is my favorite subject. **Each** boy admires his teacher. **Both** the teacher **and** the students enjoyed the class. You can have **either** tea or coffee. It is **not only** beautiful **but (also)** useful.
	2 부사	
	3 전치사	
	4 접속사	I may stop by tomorrow **or** just phone you. Both the teacher **and** the students enjoyed the class.
III. 문장의 구조	1 문장성분의 기초	You can **put the dish on the table**. He **gave me a present**. They **elected him president**.
	2 문장의 형식	
	3 평서문의 전환	
	4 의문문의 비교	**Have you** finished your homework yet? This is your book, **isn't it**?
IV. 문장의 시제	1 단순시제	I **will be** able to help you get to the party tonight. **Are you going** to take the last train?
	2 진행시제	**I'm thinking** about the problem. I **was studying** when John called me.
	3 현재완료	The bakery **has been** open since 1960. He **has attended** the club meetings regularly.
	4 시간을 나타내는 접속사	**Since** he left this morning, I haven't seen him. **When** we arrived, she was talking on the phone.
V. to부정사와 동명사	1 to부정사	**To see** is **to belive**. Chris was glad **to hear the news**.
	2 동명사	We **enjoy swimming** in the pool. Life is **worth living**. I'm interested in **watching horror movies**.
	3 to부정사와 동명사 비교	
	4 의미상주어	It is difficult **for me to speak French**. It was kind **of you to help us**.
VI. 비교급과 최상급	1 비교급과 최상급의 규칙 변화	They've got **more/less** money **than** they need. A car is **much more** expensive **than** a motorbike.
	2 비교급과 최상급의 불규칙 변화	
	3 원급의 비교	You can run **as fast as** Billy can. She is old, but she is not **as old as** he (is).
	4 최상급의 비교	Cindy is **the shortest** of the three. It is **the most interesting** speech I've ever heard.

High Junior Syllabus

High Junior		2015 개정 중등 영어 언어형식
Chapter	**Unit**	
I. 문장의 형성	1 8품사와 문장 성분	**The audience** is/are enjoying the show. I'd like to **write a diary**, but I'm too busy to do so. He**'s being** very rude. We **are hoping** you will be with us.
	2 문장의 형식	
	3 문장의 배열	I think **(that)** he is a good actor. **Although/Though** it was cold, I went swimming.
	4 문장의 강조	The weather was **so** nice **that** we went hiking. **It was Justin who/that** told me the truth.
II 부정사와 동명사	1 원형부정사	You shouldn't **let** him **go** there again. I **heard** the children **sing/singing**.
	2 to부정사	He seemed **to have been ill (for some time)**. Bill promised Jane **to work out with her**. I remembered **John/John's coming late for class**. It goes without **saying that time is money**. There is no use **crying over the spilt milk**.
	3 동명사	
	4 to부정사와 동명사구	
III. 분사	1 현재분사	At the station I met a lady **carrying a large umbrella**. **With the night coming**, stars began to shine in the sky.
	2 과거분사	Wallets **found on the street** must be reported to the police.
	3 분사구문	**Walking along the street,** I met an old friend. **Having seen that movie before,** I wanted to see it again.
	4 독립분사구문	**Joshua returning home,** the puppy ran toward him. **Frankly speaking,** I failed the test.
IV. 수동태	1 수동태의 형성	The building **was built** in 1880. I **was made** to clean the room. Nolan **was seen** to enter the building. The monkey **has been raised** by human parents for years. Cooper **will be invited** to today's meeting. The information superhighway **will have been introduced** to everyone by 2015.
	2 수동태와 능동태의 전환	
	3 수동태와 전치사의 사용	
	4 주의해야 할 수동태 용법	
V. 관계대명사와 관계부사	1 관계대명사의 사용	The girl **who is playing the piano** is called Ann. This is the book **(that) I bought yesterday**.
	2 관계대명사와 선행사	Please tell me **what happened**.
	3 관계대명사의 생략	This is **why** we have to study English grammar.
	4 관계부사	The town **in which I was born** is very small. That's just **how he talks**, always serious about his work.
VI. 가정법	1 가정법 현재와 과거	**If it were not for you, I would** be lonely.
	2 가정법 과거완료	**Had** I had enough money, I **would have bought** a cell phone. **Without/But for** your advice, I **would have** failed.
	3 혼합가정법	I **wish** I **had learned** swimming last summer. He acts **as if** he **had been** there.
	4 특수가정법	I'd **rather** we **had** dinner now. **Provided that/As long as** they had plenty to eat, the crew **seemed** to be happy.

CHAPTER 01

I. 문장의 형성

UNIT 01

8품사와 문장성분

개념

① **명사:** 사람이나 사물의 이름을 가리키는 말

② **대명사:** 사람이나 사물의 이름을 대신하여 가리키는 말

③ **형용사:** 사람이나 사물의 모양이나 성질을 나타내는 말

④ **동사:** 주어의 동작이나 상태를 나타내는 말

⑤ **부사:** 장소, 시간, 방법, 이유 등을 나타내는 말

⑥ **전치사:** 문장 속 다른 요소와의 관계를 나타내는 말

⑦ **접속사:** 단어, 구, 절을 연결하는 말

⑧ **감탄사:** 놀람, 느낌, 부름, 응답 등을 나타내는 말

쓰임

주어, 목적어, 보어, 수식어, 서술어 등 문장성분으로 쓰일 때

① **주어 역할:** 명사, 대명사

② **목적어 역할:** 명사, 대명사

③ **보어 역할:** 명사, 대명사, 형용사

④ **수식어 역할:** 부사

⑤ **서술어 역할:** 동사

8품사와 문장성분

명사	**주어** The **light bulb** was invented by Edison. 주어(관사 + 명사)
	목적어 TEAT manufactures **electric cars**. 목적어
	보어 Jessi is **an astronaut**. 보어(관사 + 명사)
대명사	**주어** **They** are the students whom Eric met. 주어
	목적어 There is a box. Kittens love **it**. 목적어
	보어 That smart phone is **mine**. 보어
형용사	**수식어** **Beautiful** flowers bloom in Spring. 수식어
	보어 You may not understand me, but she's **cute**. 보어

동사	^{서술어} I <u>wish</u> to receive a present from Wendy. 　　　서술어
부사	^{수식어} The boy speaks English <u>easily</u>. 　　　　　　　　　　　수식어
전치사	Everyone <u>in</u> the room saw the man dancing. 　　　　　전치사
접속사	John was surprised to hear <u>that</u> she had left. 　　　　　　　　　　　　접속사
감탄사	<u>Hurrah</u>! We have no lesson today! 감탄사

Exercise

 ## Exercise 1

둘 중 맞는 단어를 골라 문장을 완성하세요.

① How come this milk has gone bad so **quick / quickly** ?

② My best friend is surprised at **her / hers** phone's high technology.

③ Nana has **created / creation** the most wonderful artwork among us.

④ There are many people **on / at** the station.

⑤ It is **help / helpful** to pause and see it from a different view.

 ## Exercise 2

주어진 단어들을 바르게 배열해 문장을 완성하세요.

① 내 꿈은 세계적으로 유명한 작가가 되는 것이다.

→ _____ .

(to become, a world-renowned, is, my dream, author)

② 그는 경제가 회복될 것이라고 굳게 믿고 있다.

→ _____ .

(the economy, that, he has, firm belief, will recover)

③ 사람들이 왜 그렇게 빠르게 달리고 있는지 아니?

→ _____ ?

(why, have any idea, you, so fast, do, people are running)

 Exercise 3

빈칸을 채워 문장을 완성하세요.

① 그들의 다가올 새학년 계획은 올해의 팀 상을 따내는 것이다.

           plan for the upcoming school year is to win the Best Team Award.

② 나는 Ben의 여자형제를 몇 번 봤지만, 그녀를 잘 모른다.

I've met Ben's sister a few times, but I don't know her　　　　　　　.

③ 특별한 이유가 있지 않은 한 지원서를 제 시간에 제출해야 한다.

You have to submit your application on time　　　　　　　 you have a special reason.

④ 이런, 내가 이미 보낸 이메일에서 치명적인 실수를 찾았어.

          , I found a critical mistake in the email I already sent.

⑤ 너는 네 택배를 영업일 기준으로 10일 내에 받을 것이다.

You will receive your delivery　　　　　　　 10 business days.

⑥ 크리스마스는 세계의 많은 나라들에 의해 기념된다.

Christmas is celebrated　　　　　　　 many countries all over the world.

Sentence Completion

1 He sent a _____ to the neighbor who makes terrible noise past midnight.

(A) notify
(B) notice
(C) notified
(D) notices

2 The _____ was an innovative discovery in the 20th century which changed human life today.

(A) internet
(B) invisible
(C) introduce
(D) international

3 Among the gift boxes on the desk, the green one with the red dots is _____.

(A) you
(B) your
(C) yours
(D) you're

4 If you cheat on your assignments, your punishment will be _____.

(A) swift
(B) swifts
(C) swiftly
(D) swifting

5 Everyone in this room is suffering from an _____ odor from an unknown source.

(A) awe
(B) awful
(C) awfully
(D) awesome

6 Intimidated by his look, my little sister was _____ to talk to her new tutor.

(A) afraid
(B) scary
(C) fearless
(D) nervously

7 These new magnifiers _____ objects ten times bigger than they actually are.

(A) large

(B) larger

(C) enlarge

(D) enlarging

8 _____ the meeting perfectly twenty minutes ahead so that it will proceed smoothly.

(A) Prepare

(B) Prepared

(C) Preparing

(D) To prepare

9 Surprisingly, Sandy finished this time-consuming homework _____ than anyone else in our class.

(A) easy

(B) easier

(C) more easily

(D) the most easily

10 He was _____ disappointed that he did not win the prize.

(A) bitter

(B) bitters

(C) bitterly

(D) bittering

11 Gwen realized _____ has always been the first to come to the meeting.

(A) she that

(B) that she

(C) who she

(D) she been

12 Will Hailey come to the farewell party _____ is on her working day?

(A) even though

(B) even though it

(C) it even though

(D) even though not

Error Recognition

● TOSEL 기출문제 변형 수능/내신 출제유형

 틀린 문장 고르기

다음 중 문법적으로 <u>틀린</u> 것을 고르세요.

We had a group project about how honey is made. I thought doing a group project was going to be ❶ fun . The teacher said we would have a great time. But doing group work was ❷ awful . First of all, our group scheduled a meeting after school. But two members in our group cancelled ❸ sudden . Only two of us were at the meeting. Then it got worse. At the meeting, ❹ we divided up the jobs for the project. Suji's job was to research the life cycle of bees. The deadline to finish her part was last Friday. But she didn't do it! She said she was too ❺ busy . Then, Martin, another group member, got sick. The project is due on Monday, and I am doing everything myself!

 고쳐쓰기

틀린 문장의 번호를 쓰고 올바르게 고치세요.

● TOSEL 기출문제 변형 수능/내신 출제유형

✏️ 틀린 문장 고르기

다음 중 문법적으로 <u>틀린</u> 것을 고르세요.

Noura had had enough of the city. She could not stand the **①** **noisy** traffic, the smoggy air, the tall buildings, and the crowded sidewalks near her apartment. She **②** **needed** to get away! So she called up her cousin, Mo, who lived alone in a mountain village, and asked if she could stay with him for three days. "Of course!" said Mo. "Come on over." So Noura packed her bags and set off for Mo's. **③** **As** soon as Noura got to Mo's house, she noticed something amazing. "It is so quiet!" she said. But that night, Noura began to hear a loud sound. At first, she thought it was a dog. But then she **④** **realized** : wolves! It started with one wolf. Then there was a chorus. After a sleepless night with a pillow over her **⑤** **headed** , Noura headed right back to the familiar noise of the city.

✏️ 고쳐쓰기

틀린 문장의 번호를 쓰고 올바르게 고치세요.

➡️ _____

배운 내용 스스로 정리해보기

8품사와 문장성분

영어의 8품사들이 문장 속에서 ❶ _____, ❷ _____, ❸ _____, ❹ _____, ❺ _____ 등의 문장성분을 이루어 하나의 문장이 완성된다.

예시문장 써보기

❶ 명사 ➡ _____

❷ 대명사 ➡ _____

❸ 형용사 ➡ _____

❹ 동사 ➡ _____

❺ 부사 ➡ _____

❻ 주어가 대명사인 문장 ➡ _____

❼ 목적어가 명사인 문장 ➡ _____

❽ 보어가 형용사인 문장 ➡ _____

❾ 수식어가 부사인 문장 ➡ _____

❿ 서술어가 포함된 문장 ➡ _____

UNIT 02

문장의 형식

개념 **1** **1형식:** 주어 + 완전자동사 (S + V)

2 **2형식:** 주어 + 불완전자동사 + 보어 (S + V + S.C)

3 **3형식:** 주어 + 타동사 + 목적어 (S + V + O)

4 **4형식:** 주어 + 수여동사 + 간접목적어 + 직접목적어
(S + V + I.O + D.O)

5 **5형식:** 주어+타동사+목적어+목적격보어
(S + V + O + O.C)

쓰임 **정확한 영어 문장을 사용할 때**

ex) She let her dog. (X)
She let her dog play. (O)

ex) 4형식 I sent you a letter.
3형식 I sent a letter to you.

① 문장의 기본 형식

모든 문장은 주어와 동사를 하나씩 가진다.

1형식	The puppy runs. 　　주어　　　동사
2형식	Shawn is an artist. 　주어　동사　주격보어
3형식	He attended the meeting. 주어　동사　　　목적어
4형식	Lisa gave Judy an umbrella. 주어　동사　간접목적어　직접목적어
5형식	I found him a good boy. 주어　동사　목적어　　목적보어

② 4형식의 3형식으로의 전환

❶ 전치사 to를 취하는 동사: 주다, 보내다

4형식 I owe Victoria my success.
3형식 = I owe my success **to** Victoria.

4형식 I paid him 10 dollars.
3형식 = I paid 10 dollars **to** him.

❷ 전치사 for를 취하는 동사: 배려, 주선

4형식 He bought me a watch.
3형식 = He bought a watch **for** me.

4형식 Can you find me a bigger one?
3형식 = Can you find a bigger one **for** me?

NOTE ✎

TIP 문장의 기본 형식

- 1형식 (S + V)
- 2형식 (S + V + S.C)
- 3형식 (S + V + O)
- 4형식 (S + V + I.O + D.O)
- 5형식 (S + V + O + O.C)

TIP 전치사 to를 취하는 동사

단어	뜻
bring	가져오다
deny	부인하다
give	주다
lend	빌려주다
offer	제의하다
pay	지불하다
promise	약속하다
recommend	추천하다
sell	팔다
send	보내다
show	보여주다
teach	가르치다
write	쓰다

TIP 전치사 for를 취하는 동사

단어	뜻
buy	사다
choose	고르다
cook	요리하다
find	찾다
get	구하다
keep	유지하다
make	만들다
order	주문하다
prepare	준비하다
reach	집어주다
reserve	예약하다
spare	할애하다

❸ 5형식으로 쓰이는 동사

❶ believe형

I **believe** him (to be) honest.
　　동사　목적어　　　목적보어

I **considered** the matter as[to be] settled.
　　동사　　　목적어　　　　목적보어

❷ call형

They **called** him a liar.
　　동사　목적어 목적보어

Tony **named** the artificial intelligence(AI) Jarvis.
　　동사　　　　목적어　　　　　　목적보어

❸ make형

Her efforts **made** her the world's best mathematician.
　　　　동사　목적어　　　목적보어

They **let** the prisoner free.
　　동사　　목적어　　목적보어

❹ ask형

I **asked** her to do the dishes.
　동사　목적어　　목적보어

Sarah **allowed** her daughter to dye her hair.
　　동사　　　목적어　　　　목적보어

➡ **5형식으로 쓸 수 없는 동사**

that절을 목적어로 취한다.

- I propose that you (should) go there.

≠ I propose you to go there. (X)

NOTE ✎

TIP 목적보어의 다양한 형태

❶ 명사(구·절)·대명사
His wealth made him what he is.

❷ 형용사(구)
They beat him black and blue.

❸ 부정사
We expect you to finish the work.

❹ 현재분사
I want him attending the party.

❺ 과거분사
I want it finished by Monday.

❻ (to be) + 형용사·명사
I know him to be reliable.

❼ as + 명사·동명사·형용사·분사
He recognized him as his son.

❽ for + 목적보어
I mistook him for my friend.

TIP 5형식으로 쓸 수 없는 동사

단어	뜻
demand	요구하다
hope	희망하다
insist	주장하다
propose	
say	제안하다
suggest	

Exercise

 ### Exercise 1

둘 중 맞는 단어를 골라 문장을 완성하세요.

① Everyone in my family   calls / calls to   my brother a big baby.

② Hannah made a birthday cake   to me / for me .

③ She suggested   that I / me to   wipe the tables.

④ Don't make   I / me   yell at you for your faults.

⑤ Our teacher bought   us pizza / pizza us   at a Christmas party.

 ### Exercise 2

다음 4형식 문장을 3형식으로 전환하세요.

① The school offered Jack a full scholarship.

➡ _____.

② I'm planning to cook my best friend a French dish.

➡ _____.

③ Could you get me something to drink?

➡ _____?

④ Gary hasn't sent the professor the important email yet.

➡ _____.

⑤ Ms. Jarrett taught me how to play the guitar.

➡ _____.

 Exercise 3

빈칸을 채워 문장을 완성하세요.

① 그것이 완성되면, 나는 내가 처음으로 손뜨개질한 모자를 그녀에게 보여주고 싶다.

When it is finished, I would love to show _____ my first hand-knitted hat.

② 너에게 남은 목도리가 있다면 나에게 한 개 빌려줄 수 있니?

Could you lend _____ one of your scarves if you have any extra?

③ 나는 너를 내 새로 개조된 부엌에 초대해서 저녁을 요리해주고 싶다.

I would like to invite you to my newly renovated kitchen and cook dinner _____ you.

④ Diana 선생님께서 영국문학을 고등학생들에게 가르쳐보신 적이 있니?

Has Ms. Diana ever taught British Literature _____ high school students before?

⑤ Anthony가 충분히 자격이 있다고 생각되어서, 우리는 그를 학급장으로 임명했다.

Anthony is thought to be well-qualified, so we appointed _____ a class representative.

⑥ (만약) 모든 일이 잘 이루어지면, 이 프로젝트가 너를 팀장으로 만들어줄 것이다.

If everything goes well, this project will make _____ the team leader.

Sentence Completion

① Heather gave [   ] one of her umbrellas because it was raining a lot outside.

(A) me

(B) to me

(C) for me

(D) with me

④ Please [   ] your sister my message to meet at five o'clock here.

(A) to

(B) give

(C) to give

(D) give to

② Eating a balanced meal [   ] one of the most important things for maintaining good health.

(A) be

(B) is

(C) to be

(D) being

⑤ Victor [   ] me his collection of coins which he has collected from around the world.

(A) showed

(B) showing

(C) showed to

(D) showing to

③ He [   ] the wallet that I had lost several weeks ago, so I was so relieved.

(A) found me

(B) found my

(C) found to me

(D) found for me

⑥ I decided to sell my calculator [   ] my neighbor because I'm not using it anymore.

(A) of

(B) at

(C) to

(D) for

7 Last night when he came back home, my father brought a box of chocolate _____ us.

(A) of

(B) at

(C) to

(D) for

8 The doctor recommended vitamin B and D _____ because I lack certain nutritions.

(A) to me

(B) for me

(C) that me

(D) which me

9 Soon you will _____ much easier than when you first started it.

(A) find

(B) find it

(C) find which

(D) which find

10 You should not keep the important guests _____ for too long outside.

(A) waiting

(B) is waiting

(C) has waited

(D) that waited

11 Why would you _____ your little sister a little chubby? She is not that fat.

(A) call

(B) call to

(C) call for

(D) calling

12 Everyone believed _____ because he has built up trust for a long time.

(A) he honest

(B) his honest

(C) him honest

(D) has honest

Error Recognition

 틀린 문장 고르기

다음 중 문법적으로 <u>틀린</u> 것을 고르세요.

In the world today, around two major tsunamis occur each year.

① **Their** waves can reach heights of 30 meters. However, these tsunamis are not always easy to detect in advance.

② **In the middle** of the ocean, some tsunamis can be just 30 centimeters high, so sailors on ships sometimes do not even notice when a tsunami has passed right **③** **under them** . However, even such low-height tsunamis travel quickly in the ocean. They can move as fast as a jet airplane, with speeds of up to 800 km/hr. These speeds **④** **allow for** tsunamis to cross an entire ocean in one day. Once a tsunami hits shallow water, the top of its waves will gain height **⑤** **extremely** quickly.

 고쳐쓰기

틀린 문장의 번호를 쓰고 올바르게 고치세요.

⟶ _____

● TOSEL 기출문제 변형 수능/내신 출제유형

틀린 문항 고르기

다음 중 문법적으로 <u>틀린</u> 것을 고르세요.

Many people believe that we need to be fully awake to solve difficult problems. However, many difficult problems ❶ **require** creativity. Some scientists have found that being a bit sleepy can actually help with creativity. In one experiment, a scientist ❷ **gave to** university students different kinds of problems to solve. The first kind of problem was about analysis. ❸ **These** problems looked like math questions from a test. The second kind of problem required students ❹ **to think** creative. For example, they would have to think up different uses for a spoon. For the analysis problems, being sleepy or wide awake made no difference to the students' scores. However, for the problems ❺ **that** needed creative thinking, the students got better scores when they were a little tired.

고쳐쓰기

틀린 문장의 번호를 쓰고 올바르게 고치세요.

✏️ 배운 내용 스스로 정리해보기

① 문장의 기본형식

모든 문장은 **❶** _____ 와(과) **❷** _____ 를 하나씩 가지며 총 **❸** _____ 개의
형식으로 나뉜다.

예시문장 써보기

❶ 1형식 ➜ _____

❷ 2형식 ➜ _____

❸ 3형식 ➜ _____

❹ 4형식 ➜ _____

❺ 5형식 ➜ _____

② 4형식의 3형식으로의 전환

❶ _____ 문장은 **❷** _____ 문장으로 전환이 가능하다. 단 **❸** _____ 문장으로 전환

될 때 알맞은 **❹** _____ 을(를) 삽입해야 한다.

예시문장 써보기

❶ 전치사 to를 취하는 동사가 사용된 4형식 문장

➜ _____

❷ 전치사 to를 취하는 동사가 사용된 3형식 문장

➜ _____

③ 5형식으로 쓰이는 동사

5형식으로 쓰이는 동사의 종류에는 **❶** believe형, **❷** call형, **❸** _____ 형, **❹** ask형 등이
있고 반대로 5형식으로 쓸 수 없는 동사도 있다.

예시문장 써보기

❶ _____ 형 ➜ _____

❷ 5형식으로 쓰일 수 없는 문장 ➜ _____

UNIT 03

문장의 배열

UNIT **3** 문장의 배열

① 형용사의 어순

한정사	기수	주관적평가	크기·형상	성질·상태	신구·연령	색채	재료·소속	명사
the	two	typical	large				Korean	houses
a						grey		tower
some		intricate			old		Chinese	designs
his				heavy	new	purple		wallet

The <u>four</u> <u>small</u> <u>white</u> <u>kittens</u> are sleeping in the box.
한정사 기수   크기   색채   명사

② 부사의 어순

① 형용사를 수식하는 경우

She is a <u>very</u> <u>astute</u> woman.
         부사   형용사

② 부사·부사구·부사절을 수식하는 경우

He knows it <u>perfectly</u> <u>well</u>.
             부사   부사

③ 문장 전체를 수식하는 경우

<u>Certainly</u> <u>he will come</u>.
  부사   문장

③ 문장을 길게 만드는 접속사

that	<u>That</u> <u>he</u> <u>is</u> a genius <u>is</u> unbelievable. 접속사 주어 동사 동사
for	The <u>game</u> <u>was called off</u> <u>for</u> <u>it</u> <u>rained</u> heavily. 주어 동사 접속사 비인칭주어 동사
whereas	I <u>prefer</u> black tea <u>whereas</u> <u>Julia</u> <u>prefers</u> coffee. 주어 동사 접속사 주어 동사

NOTE

TIP 한정사의 종류

① 관사(a, an, the)
② 지시형용사(this, that, these, those)
③ 부정형용사(another, some, any…)
④ 수량형용사(many, much, few…)
⑤ 관계형용사(which, what…)
⑥ 의문형용사(which, what, whose…)

TIP that을 생략할 수 있는 경우

• that절이 회화체로 흔히 쓰이는 'think, say, shout, know, suppose, imagine, hope, wish, expect, believe'등의 목적어일 때 that을 생략할 수 있음.
She said <u>(that)</u> she wanted to go home.

I believe <u>(that)</u> we'll be able to help them.

TIP that을 생략할 수 없는 경우

• that절이 문어체로 흔히 쓰이는 'assume, admit, agree, state, assert, report, hold, learn, maintain, suggest, reckon'등의 목적어일 때 that을 생략할 수 없음.
She mentioned that she wanted to get drunk.

The policeman maintained that he acted alone in the shooting.

④ 문장을 길게 만드는 전치사

❶ 방향·장소

There is no one <u>in</u> the room.

We met <u>at</u> the bus stop.

He was born <u>at</u> 36 Orange County.

There's a dirty mark <u>on</u> the wall.

❷ 시간

The school opened <u>in</u> 1940 with only nine students.

Perry usually go home <u>at</u> 10 o'clock.

We'll go on a date <u>on</u> Sunday [<u>on</u> my birthday].

I've not seen him <u>for</u> three days.

<u>During</u> the night the rain changed to snow.

He has been ill <u>since</u> last Monday.

He works <u>from</u> 9 a.m. to 5 p.m.

⑤ 접속사와 전치사의 비교

❶ 접속사(although / (even) though) vs. 전치사(despite / in spite of)

<u>[Al]though</u> he made efforts, he failed to win the first prize.
= <u>Despite[In spite of]</u> his efforts, he failed to win the first prize.

❷ 접속사(rather than) vs. 전치사(rather than / instead of)

James will run to school <u>rather than</u> ride a bicycle.
<u>Rather than[instead of]</u> watching a movie, he studied math.

Exercise

 ## Exercise 1

둘 중 맞는 단어를 골라 문장을 완성하세요.

❶ It's hard for me to stop by at the bank for / during the day.

❷ I've been waiting for 20 minutes for the bus on / at the bus stop.

❸ In / On 2020, a contagious disease was spread all over the world.

❹ Everyone complained about the cold air in / at the meeting room.

❺ There have been some technical issues with my desktop for / since last week.

 ## Exercise 2

주어진 단어들을 바르게 배열해 문장을 완성하세요.

❶ 옆집에 성질이 급한 키가 크고 나이든 여자가 있다.

➜ _____ .

   (next door, old, there is, a, woman, hot-tempered, tall)

❷ 이 상황은 명백히 그녀의 실수 때문에 발생했다.

➜ _____ .

   (because of, obviously, occurred, her mistake, this situation)

❸ 인터넷이 서버 점검으로 너무 느리다.

➜ _____ .

   (server inspection, too, the internet, slow, is, due to)

Exercise 3

주어진 단어를 활용하여 빈칸을 채워 문장을 완성하세요.

① 안타깝게도, 내가 그 다리 아래에서 구조했던 강아지가 살아나지 못했다.

＿＿＿＿＿＿, the dog I had rescued under the bridge didn't make it. (unfortunate)

② 그녀의 귀여운 외모에도 불구하고 사람들은 그녀의 나쁜 성격 때문에 그녀를 피한다.

＿＿＿＿＿＿ her cute appearance, people avoid her due to her bad temper. (spite)

③ 타이타닉이라고 불리는 영국 증기선이 빙하 때문에 가라앉았다.

The British steamboat called Titanic sank ＿＿＿＿＿＿ an iceberg. (because)

④ 내가 생각하기에 그의 최근 행동으로 볼 때 Salt씨가 완전히 우리의 편인 것 같다.

I think Mr. Salt is ＿＿＿＿＿＿ on our side judging from his recent behavior. (definite)

⑤ Tom이 직장을 잃었고 그의 부인이 그를 떠났기 때문에 나는 그가 걱정됐다.

I was worried about Tom ＿＿＿＿＿＿ he lost his job and his wife left him. (because)

⑥ 그 영화가 너무 재미있어서 그것이 너무 빠르게 끝났다고 느껴졌다.

The movie was so interesting that it felt like it ended too ＿＿＿＿＿＿. (quick)

Sentence Completion

1 Jannet wore a ▒▒▒▒▒ dress, and it matched her beautiful eyes.

(A) nice blue new

(B) new nice blue

(C) nice new blue

(D) blue nice new

2 Harry bought his new car from a ▒▒▒▒▒ car brand.

(A) famous German

(B) German famous

(C) famously German

(D) German famously

3 Kate bought this house ▒▒▒▒▒ because it was right next to her mother's house.

(A) just

(B) even

(C) simple

(D) enough

4 He ▒▒▒▒▒ shook his hands with Mrs. White, accepting the offer she made.

(A) firm

(B) firmly

(C) firming

(D) firmed

5 It was certain ▒▒▒▒▒ the thief entered through the window.

(A) for

(B) that

(C) because

(D) whereas

6 My mother likes swimming ▒▒▒▒▒ my father likes hiking.

(A) for

(B) that

(C) whereas

(D) in spite of

7 She must have been very tired, _____ she fell asleep immediately.

(A) for
(B) that
(C) despite
(D) whereas

8 My arms were in a cast _____ three weeks.

(A) in
(B) at
(C) for
(D) during

9 _____ December 18th 1865, the Thirteenth Amendment was approved.

(A) In
(B) At
(C) On
(D) From

10 When I asked an old man how to get to the bus stop, he only pointed me the direction _____ saying to me.

(A) for
(B) despite
(C) in spite of
(D) rather than

11 _____ he couldn't win a medal, Ted was proud of himself for not giving up.

(A) As
(B) Despite
(C) Although
(D) In Spite of

12 The airplane to Busan landed perfectly _____ foggy weather.

(A) though
(B) despite
(C) although
(D) instead of

Error Recognition

 틀린 문장 고르기

다음 중 문법적으로 <u>틀린</u> 것을 고르세요.

At Grandpa's house, there is always an ① **extremely giant** jigsaw puzzle on the table. On Monday, Grandpa and Maria decided to finish one puzzle ② **in** two days. It was a major task because the puzzle had 1000 pieces. First, they put all the edge pieces together. Doing this meant looking carefully through all the pieces. ③ **Since** Grandpa has poor eyesight, Maria did this part. Once the edges ④ **were done** , they divided pieces into groups by color. Dark blue pieces went to the left. Light blue pieces were on the right. And a lot of white pieces went at the top for sorting. There were many ⑤ **white tiny** pieces because the puzzle was a picture of a cloudy sky. They put all the pieces together by Tuesday night. It was a fun challenge, but Maria did not want to do another puzzle for a long time.

 고쳐쓰기

틀린 문장의 번호를 쓰고 올바르게 고치세요.

➡ _____

High Junior Book 1 UNIT 3 문장의 배열

 틀린 문장 고르기

● TOSEL 기출문제 변형 수능/내신 출제유형

다음 중 문법적으로 <u>틀린</u> 것을 고르세요.

Wild anteaters live in Central and South America. They live in a variety of habitats, including grasslands and rainforests. They are unusual and fascinating animals. One of the most interesting things about anteaters ❶ is how they eat. They have no teeth. Instead, they have a ❷ long sticky tongue to catch ants and termites. An anteater's tongue can be up to 600 cm long. Anteaters move their tongue really ❸ quick to catch the ants. The tongue moves 150 times a minute so that ants cannot bite the anteater. The long tongue of an anteater is inside the animal's ❹ long nose. An anteater uses its long nose and great sense of smell to find its food. It pokes its nose ❺ into the holes on top of anthills in order to suck out ants. However, anteaters avoid destroying anthills. They might go back to the same place for their next meal.

 고쳐쓰기

틀린 문장의 번호를 쓰고 올바르게 고치세요.

High Junior Book 1   49

 배운 내용 스스로 정리해보기

① 형용사의 어순

여러개의 형용사가 배열되는 경우 ❶ [   ], ❷ [   ], ❸ [   ],
❹ [   ], ❺ [   ], ❻ [   ], ❼ [   ] 의 순서대로 나열한다.

예시문장 써보기
large, two, beautiful, new를 사용하기

→ _____

② 부사의 어순

부사는 수식하는 어구 ❶ [   ] 또는 ❷ [   ] 에 위치한다.

③ 문장을 길게 만드는 접속사

접속사는 한 문장 안에 ❶ [   ] 이(가) ❷ [   ] 개 이상 올 수 있게 만든다.

예시문장 써보기
that을 사용한 문장 → _____

④ 문장을 길게 만드는 전치사

전치사 for은 ❶ [   ] 으(로) 표현된 기간, during은 명사로 표현된 기간과 함께 사용된다.
전치사 ❷ [   ] 은(는) 어느 시점 이후 계속, ❸ [   ] 은(는) 때 또는 순서의 기점을
의미한다.

예시문장 써보기
for를 사용한 문장 → _____

⑤ 접속사와 전치사의 비교

접속사 뒤에는 ❶ [   ] 이(가) 오고 전치사 뒤에는 ❷ [   ] 이(가) 온다.

예시문장 써보기
❶ 접속사가 사용된 문장 → _____

❷ 전치사가 사용된 문장 → _____

UNIT 04

문장의 강조

개념 내용상 강조되는 문장의 구성성분을 두드러지게 보이기 위해
변형된 특수한 구문들이다.

1 도치구문: 강조되는 목적어, 보어, 부사(구) 등을 앞으로
보내고 뒤의 주어와 동사의 위치를 도치

2 so-that 결과구문: so + 형용사 + 동사 + 주어 + that…'
의 형태로 '너무-해서…하다.'로 해석

3 It-that 강조구문: 'It + be + ... + that'의 형태로 주어,
명사보어, 목적어, 부사를 강조

4 재귀대명사의 강조적 용법: 주어, 보어, 목적어를 강조할
때 쓰이며 대부분 생략 가능

5 비교급과 최상급의 강조: 비교급과 최상급을 더 강조할 때
쓰이며 각각에 알맞은 강조부사를 사용

UNIT ④ 문장의 강조

❶ 도치구문

목적어	Really good desserts they made at the restaurant. 목적어 주어 동사 Not a word did he say all day long. 목적어 동사 주어
보어	Happy is the child who is content with his score. 보어 동사 주어 Very grateful they were for your help. 보어 주어(대명사) 동사
부사(구)	Here comes the bus. 부사 동사 주어 Never shall I forget your kindness. 부정의 부사 조동사 주어

NOTE ✎

TIP 목적어가 부정어인 도치

● 목적어가 부정어이면 강조할때 주어와 동사의 순서를 바꿈.

TIP 주어가 대명사인 도치구문

● 주어가 대명사이고 보어를 강조할 때 주어와 동사의 순서를 유지함.

❷ so-that, such that 결과구문

So surprised was she that she could hardly speak.
          동사   주어

Such was his anxiety that he lost his health.
      동사   주어

❸ It-that 강조구문

She met him at the park yesterday.
= It was she that[who] met him at the park yesterday.
= It was him that[whom] she met at the park yesterday.
= It was at the park that[where] she met him yesterday.
= It was yesterday that[when] she met him at the park.

➜ not ~until 구문의 강조형

• It is **not until** we lose health **that** we know the value of it.
= **Not until[only after]** we lose health do we know the value of it.
                                  조동사 주어

= We do **not** know the value of health **until** we lose it.

TIP not-until 구문

● 'It is/was not until A that B'라고 할 때 'B한 것은 A이후이다'라고 해석할 수 있음.

④ 재귀대명사의 강조적 용법

The town (itself) was so small that it didn't have a priest.

I am not a particularly punctual person.

= I **myself** am not a particularly punctual person.
= I am not a particularly punctual person **myself**.
= **Myself**, I am not a particularly punctual person.

→ **4형식 문장에서 간접목적어를 강조할 경우 재귀대명사의 위치는 제한적이다.**

- I gave Tom **himself** a dollar.

≠ I gave Tom a dollar **himself**. (X)

⑤ 비교급과 최상급의 강조

❶ 비교급 강조

Russia is a lot bigger than any other states.

The computer she bought is a bit more expensive than mine.

❷ 최상급 강조

Being healthy is the very most important thing to me.

He is only the kindest person in our school.

TIP 비교급 강조 부사
- even, much, still, far, a lot, a bit

TIP 최상급 강조 부사
- 'the 최상급' 앞 - much, by far, only 등
- 'the와 최상급 사이' - very 등
- 'the 최상급' 뒤 - by far, ever, yet 등

Exercise

 ## Exercise 1

둘 중 맞는 단어를 고르세요.

1 The most fascinating   it is project / **project it is**   of all.

2 Excited   **the students are** / are the students   for going on a field trip.

3 Never   I did / **did I**   complete the assignment on time at every science class.

4 It was   **he that** / that he   stole my wallet when I was distracted by touts.

5 The supervisor told us   ourselves his holiday / **his holiday ourselves** .

 ## Exercise 2

밑줄 친 부분이 강조되도록 주어진 단어들을 바르게 배열해 문장을 완성하세요

1 <u>Tim 옆에는</u> 오늘 다른 학교로 전학 갈 그의 친구가 있다.

→ _____.

(his friend, will transfer, beside Tim, to the other school today, who, is)

2 세계 2차대전이 발발한 때는 <u>1938년 이후</u>이다.

→ _____.

(not, broke out, it, World War II, 1938, until, was, that)

3 <u>내가 어제 주문했던 옷들은</u> 내가 기대했던 것보다 훨씬 더 작았다.

→ _____.

(I ordered, a lot smaller than, the clothes, yesterday, I expected, were)

 ## Exercise 3

주어진 단어를 활용하여 빈칸을 채워 문장을 완성하세요.

❶ Not a request did he _____ because of the lack of budget this month. (approve)

❷ Very _____ was my friend with her canceled appointment. (disappoint)

❸ It was not until Vincent van Gogh _____ that his work got illuminated by people. (die)

❹ On the tree next to my car _____ a black cat. (lie)

❺ Never did I _____ what had happened between them. (know)

❻ So disappointed _____ the fans that they couldn't even breathe. (be)

Sentence Completion

1 Just around the corner [____] my house.

(A) is

(B) be

(C) to be

(D) being

2 Never [____] I ever tried eating stinky fruit like a durian.

(A) do

(B) did

(C) has

(D) have

3 All kinds of special experiences [____] while I was living with my grandmother.

(A) to gain

(B) gained I

(C) I gained

(D) I gaining

4 Happy [____] those who can appreciate small things.

(A) is

(B) are

(C) to be

(D) being

5 So relieved [____] the survivors that they cried out loud when they reached outside.

(A) be

(B) was

(C) were

(D) being

6 So loud [____] the noise they made that people sitting next to them were frowning.

(A) is

(B) are

(C) was

(D) were

7 It was July second [____] he first met her and fell in love.

(A) what
(B) when
(C) which
(D) where

8 It was Jason [____] I was desperately looking for.

(A) when
(B) which
(C) whom
(D) in which

9 The city [____] was remarkable, but to me, it was like a prison without bars.

(A) itself
(B) myself
(C) herself
(D) themselves

10 Gina was proud of her son because he baked cookies [____] and gave them to her.

(A) itself
(B) himself
(C) herself
(D) themselves

11 The headphone that James bought yesterday was [____] more expensive than any other headphones.

(A) so
(B) well
(C) very
(D) much

12 Hope Diamond is the [____] most valuable diamond in the world.

(A) so
(B) very
(C) such
(D) by far

Error Recognition

● TOSEL 기출문제 변형 수능/내신 출제유형

틀린 문장 고르기

다음 중 문법적으로 <u>틀린</u> 것을 고르세요.

> While most countries these days use kilometers to measure distance, some **①** **still** use the mile. It was in ancient Rome **②** **when** the basic idea for a mile started. Back then, the Romans had a measurement unit called a "mille passum," which meant "1,000 steps." In those days, one step **③** **was measured** as five Roman feet. Therefore, an ancient Roman mile equaled 5,000 ancient Roman feet. (The measurement of a foot in those days was **④** **a bit** shorter than a foot is now.) The number of feet in a mile changed according to time and place. During Queen Elizabeth's reign in England in the 1500s, a mile became about 5,280 feet. However, England's neighbors at the time **⑤** **used** different measurements. In Scotland, miles were 5,952 feet, while in Ireland they were 6,720 feet.

고쳐쓰기

틀린 문장의 번호를 쓰고 올바르게 고치세요.

_____

● TOSEL 기출문제 변형 수능/내신 출제유형

 틀린 문장 고르기

다음 중 문법적으로 <u>틀린</u> 것을 고르세요.

> If you watch the Paralympics on TV today, you can see people who do not have legs and arms doing sports at a professional level. Some use "prosthetics", or artificial body parts, to compete and live a ❶ normal life. These prosthetics were developed slowly. The ❷ very earliest ever found is a wooden toe from Egypt from around 950 BCE. It allowed the wearer to walk and wear sandals. A ❸ very more famous example is the iron arm of Götz von Berlichingen of Germany in the 16th century. It was so well made ❹ that he could write and ride a horse with it. It was ❺ not until these were invented that people without some body parts had more comfortable life.

 고쳐쓰기

틀린 문장의 번호를 쓰고 올바르게 고치세요.

➜ _____

✎ 배운 내용 스스로 정리해보기

① 도치구문

❶ _____, ❷ _____, ❸ _____ 등이 내용상 강조되어야 할 때 이것들을 앞으로 보내고 뒤의 ❹ _____ 와(과) ❺ _____ 의 위치가 도치된다.

예시문장 써보기
부사(구) 강조 ➜ _____

② so-that 결과구문

예시문장 써보기
so-that 결과구문 ➜ _____

③ It-that 강조구문

예시문장 써보기
It-that[whom] 강조구문 ➜ _____

④ 재귀대명사의 강조적 용법

재귀대명사는 _____ 와 동격으로 쓰여 그것들을 강조한다. 강조적 용법의 재귀대명사는 생략해도 문장 구조에 지장이 없고, 위치는 자유롭다.

예시문장 써보기
He와 himself를 사용하여 영작 ➜ _____

⑤ 비교급과 최상급의 강조

비교급과 최상급을 더 강조하여 표현할때, 비교급과 최상급에 알맞은 _____ 을(를) 사용한다.

예시문장 써보기
❶ 비교급 강조 ➜ _____

❷ 최상급 강조 ➜ _____

TOSEL 실전문제 ❶

PART 6. Sentence Completion

DIRECTIONS: In this portion of the test, you will be given 12 incomplete sentences. From the choices provided, choose the word or words that correctly complete the sentence. Then, fill in the corresponding space on your answer sheet.

1.   The _____ of the lesson may change depending on how the students react.

   (A) length
   (B) lengthy
   (C) lengthen
   (D) lengthening

2.   Whose knife is _____? This should go in the knife holder on the counter.

   (A) it
   (B) its
   (C) ones
   (D) these

3.   The app provides some important tips on how to get the best _____ car.

   (A) rent
   (B) rental
   (C) renter
   (D) render

4.   All the stores will be closing at 4 p.m. _____ Friday because of the holiday.

   (A) at
   (B) in
   (C) on
   (D) among

5.   When you are indoors, wearing socks and slippers will keep your _____.

   (A) cosy
   (B) cosy feet
   (C) feet cosy
   (D) feet's cosy

6.   Emily suddenly stopped crying and smiled when her brother _____ the missing doll.

   (A) found her
   (B) her found
   (C) to find her
   (D) found to her

7. Everyone _____ a good teacher because he is very supportive of all his students.

   (A) considers us
   (B) considers him
   (C) considers to us
   (D) considers for him

8. My brother was thrilled with his gift of _____ bow ties for his clown act.

   (A) three yellow nice new big
   (B) three new nice big yellow
   (C) three nice big new yellow
   (D) three big nice yellow new

9. Those who joined the school club are asked to arrive at the auditorium _____ at 5 p.m.

   (A) prompt
   (B) prompts
   (C) promptly
   (D) prompted

10. _____ bad weather, the organizer didn't cancel the outdoor Culture Day event yesterday.

    (A) Although
    (B) In spite of
    (C) In case of
    (D) Even though

11. _____ have I experienced such a better public transportation when I travelled before.

    (A) Ever
    (B) Never
    (C) Neither
    (D) Although

12. It was at Bingwen's house _____ we first met each other to celebrate his birthday.

    (A) that
    (B) when
    (C) which
    (D) whatever

TOSEL 실전 문제

Error Recognition

● TOSEL 기출문제 변형 수능/내신 출제유형

✏️ **(1~2) 다음 중 문법적으로 틀린 것을 골라 고치세요.**

1

It is nice to give flowers to someone for love, friendship, or gratitude. Be careful **❶** **yourself** when you give flowers to someone from a different country, though. You may not be saying what you think you are. In Russia, an even number of flowers **❷** **is** only given at funerals, so if you give a Russian 12 red roses, you are telling them to die. In Japan, the sweet pea means goodbye, **❸** **so** you could be telling someone to go away! Be **❹** **especial** careful giving flowers in Mexico. Red flowers are bad luck, and yellow flowers mean death. As such, **❺** **important** is to pay attention to each country's culture when presenting flowers.

 ➡️ _____

2

Sometimes we think ❶ that humans rule the planet, but there are a lot of places where that's simply not true. ❷ In one area in Florida, snakes that were once people's pets have escaped and are running wild. People have even been killed by these former pets. In some areas, the plants that people brought from other countries ❸ have covered the entire rivers. One ant group has grown to over 500 billion members and has built homes on four continents. People often call this ❹ to ecosystem destruction . Maybe it won't be ❺ long until one of these plants or animals covers the whole world!

Error Recognition

 (3~6) 다음 중 문법적으로 틀린 것을 고르세요.

● TOSEL 기출문제 변형 수능/내신 출제유형

3

People often think ❶ that the blue whale is the biggest living thing on Earth, but that's not ❷ truly . The biggest living thing on Earth ❸ isn't an animal at all. It's a plant. Some plants are far bigger than the largest dinosaur that ever lived. There is a tree in Utah named Pando that has roots going out for 400 square kilometers. Another ❹ huge living thing, a honey mushroom in Oregon, might be even bigger. Most of it is underground, ❺ so nobody knows exactly how big it is.

● TOSEL 기출문제 변형 수능/내신 출제유형

4

Have you ever dropped your smartphone? Sometimes the screen cracks, but often the ❶ strong extra glass is ok. That's because it's not ❷ regular glass like a window, but a special type of glass called Gorilla Glass. It's used in most computers, televisions, and of course smartphones. It's made by dipping the glass in very hot salt ❸ for a moment. The temperature can be as high as 400 degrees Celsius. This makes the glass stronger ❹ so it doesn't get cracked or scratched ❺ easily .

5

All over the world, coffee is very popular ❶ **because** it can help you stay awake. This is because of the caffeine in coffee beans. In Argentina, however, they use a ❷ **different** way to stay awake. The leaves of the Yerba Mate plant also ❸ **has** caffeine. People in Argentina dry the leaves and ❹ **use** them to make a drink that is just as good as coffee. It's so popular ❺ **that** on average a person consumes about 5 kilograms of it every year.

6

During World War II, a German soldier Ulrich Steinhilper was captured and ❶ **put** in a prison in Canada. However, it was ❷ **difficult** to keep him in the prison. He escaped twice from the Canadian prison, but the third time was the most amazing. He ❸ **stole** a painter's clothes, and pretended to be painting the gate of the prison. Nobody realized ❹ **that** he wasn't a real painter, so he just kept painting the outside fence until he got far enough to just walk away. Later, people called ❺ **he** the genius of escape.

수능 대비 문제

CHAPTER 02

II. 부정사와 동명사

UNIT 01

원형부정사

<table>
<tr>
<td>생김새</td>
<td>동사원형
ex) <u>exercise</u> (O), to exercise (X), exercising (X)</td>
</tr>
<tr>
<td>쓰임</td>
<td>
❶ 5형식 문장(S + V + O + O.C)에서 사역동사의 목적격 보어로 쓰임

　ex) He <u>made</u> me <u>repeat</u> the sentences.
　　<u>Let</u> me <u>borrow</u> your books.

❷ 5형식 문장 (S + V + O + O.C)에서 지각동사의 목적격 보어로 쓰임

　ex) I <u>saw</u> you <u>study</u> in the library.
　　She <u>noticed</u> the butterfly <u>sit</u> on the flower.

❸ 조동사의 뒤에 쓰임

　ex) I <u>will</u> <u>go</u> to graduate school.
　　<u>Could</u> you <u>close</u> the window?
</td>
</tr>
</table>

❶ 지각 · 사역동사

지각동사와 사역동사의 목적격 보어는 원형부정사를 쓴다.

지각 동사	Emily <u>saw</u> the fish <u>rise</u> out of the water.
사역 동사	The teacher <u>made</u> me <u>do</u> my homework.

→ **지각동사**

see	보다	hear	듣다, 들리다
look at	...을 보다[살피다]	listen to	귀를 기울이다
watch	(관심을 갖고) 보다	feel	(감정기분이) 들다
observe	...을 보다	perceive	감지[인지]하다
know	알(게 되)다	notice	...을 의식하다

→ **사역동사**

make	(강제로 하도록) 만들다[시키다]
have	(누구에게 무엇을 하도록) 하다[시키다]
let	(...을 하도록) 허락하다

→ **준사역동사**

help	Chamomile tea <u>helps</u> people <u>(to)</u> <u>relieve</u> the tension.

NOTE ✎

TIP 감각동사

● 지각동사는 5형식, 감각동사는 2형식 문장에 사용됨. 주어와 동사의 순서를 유지함.

look	~처럼 보이다
sound	~같이 들리다
smell	~냄새가 나다
taste	~맛이 나다
feel	(감정기분이) 들다

TIP 지각동사와 현재분사(-ing)

● 지각동사가 올 때 목적어와 목적격 보어가 능동관계면 목적격보어 자리에 동사원형이나 현재분사(ing)를 쓸 수 있고, 현재분사가 올 경우는 동작의 진행을 강조할 때 씀.

❷ 조동사

원형부정사 앞에서 특정한 의미를 부여한다.

can	가능 I <u>can</u> **repair** the computer.
	허가 The audience <u>can</u> **ask** questions after the speech.
	<u>Could</u> I **have** a cup of tea? 공손한 표현의 could
may	허가 You <u>may</u> **go** home any time. 미래의 허가도 포함
	양보 Whatever Jenny <u>may</u> **say**, I will not believe her.
	추측 Fin has a fever. He <u>may</u> **go** to the hospital.
will	미래 Peter <u>will</u> **marry** Michelle.
	의지 I <u>will</u> **travel** around the world when I graduate.
must	의무 The doctor <u>must</u> **tell** the truth to the patient.
	추측 Minha <u>must</u> **be** hungry. She exercised for an hour.

→ **조동사 + have + p.p**

should have p.p	You <u>should</u> **have taken** her advice.
could have p.p	He <u>could</u> **have gone** abroad.
would have p.p	They <u>would</u> **have solved** the problem.
might have p.p	She <u>might</u> **have forgotten** to email him.
must have p.p	He <u>must</u> **have had** a crush on Emma.

NOTE 🖉

TIP **would의 관용표현**

would like to	~하고 싶다
would rather	~하는 편이 낫다
had better	

TIP **might vs. may**

- might는 may처럼 '~할지도 모른다'라는 추측의 뜻이지만, might는 확률이 낮을 때 추측의 의미로, may는 확률이 높을 때 추측의 의미로 쓰임.

TIP **should vs. must**

- should는 must처럼 '~해야 한다'라는 뜻이지만, must는 해야만 하는 의무의 뜻으로, should는 '~하는 것이 좋겠다'라는 권고의 뜻으로 쓰임

TIP **조동사 should**

- 시제 일치상 shall의 과거형임.
(의무) You should go to school.

TIP **조동사 ought to**

- should와 유사하게, 의무 나타냄.
(의무) You ought to save money.

TIP **조동사의 부정형**

- '조동사 + not'의 형태임. 단, ought to의 부정형은 ought not to임.

Exercise

 ## Exercise 1

둘 중 맞는 단어를 골라 문장을 완성하세요.

❶ I perceived my friend hold / held a grudge against me because I had missed her call.

❷ Julia heard the stranger shouted / shouting at the children.

❸ The habit of tidying my desk makes / helps me to come up with some brilliant ideas.

❹ The lecturer may / has permit students to use laptops during the class today.

❺ You must / should wait in line in order to get the food you ordered.

❻ I should read / have read the books on the shelf before I sent them to my cousins.

 ## Exercise 2

주어진 단어들을 바르게 배열해 문장을 완성하세요.

❶ 그 의사는 그녀의 환자가 과민성 대장 증후군 증상을 앓고 있다는 것을 알았다.

→ _____.

(suffer, her, the doctor, irritable, knew, colon syndrome, an, patient)

❷ 내 남동생은 주말에 스트레스 경감을 위해 휴식을 취하는 것이 낫다.

→ _____.

(had better, my brother, take some rest, on weekend, to relieve stress)

❸ 그는 온종일 숙제를 위해 관련 자료를 찾는 데 시간 보냈을지도 모른다.

→ _____.

(searching for the materials, might have, he, for assignments, the whole day, spent)

✎ Exercise 3

주어진 단어를 활용하여 빈칸을 채워 문장을 완성하세요.

❶ The actor sees his co-star _____ the script for today's filming. (memorize)

❷ One of the staff looked carefully at the customers _____ the displayed items. (touch)

❸ Driving electric vehicles helps _____ carbon emissions. (reduce)

❹ Could I _____ this contract in advance before you leave our company? (sign)

❺ The test takers who already failed once will _____ hard for next year's exam. (study)

❻ I _____ cancer from recurring if I had gotten a check-up. (prevent)

Sentence Completion

① A few people who were there saw the actress _____ the cafe and order a cup of coffee.

(A) enter

(B) entered

(C) to enter

(D) have entered

② I still remember the time when I saw countless stars _____ above my head.

(A) twinkle

(B) twinkled

(C) twinkles

(D) was twinkling

③ The referee is observing the soccer player _____ a foul during the first round of the tournament.

(A) committed

(B) to commit

(C) committing

(D) to committing

④ She noticed him _____ at her while she was in the same place with him.

(A) to star

(B) staring

(C) starring

(D) by staring

⑤ The basketball coach has his students _____ extra hours to win the next game against the most competitive team.

(A) practice

(B) practiced

(C) to practice

(D) have practiced

⑥ Our class president _____ classmates take dictation during the break time so as to finish the class earlier.

(A) has

(B) hear

(C) have

(D) hears

7 _____ him listen to the music when he takes rest after finishing all the stuff he has to do.

(A) Let

(B) Hear

(C) Know

(D) Sound

8 The facial-recognition app _____ the privacy while it can be useful for tracking criminals.

(A) may invade

(B) must invade

(C) should invade

(D) had better invade

9 I _____ learn the skills on this website than take a class every weekend.

(A) can

(B) have

(C) should

(D) would rather

10 I think you _____ skim through the manuscript before proofreading in detail.

(A) need

(B) should

(C) rather not

(D) would like

11 I _____ not red but black dress for Black Swan costume for Halloween last month.

(A) can choose

(B) will choose

(C) should choose

(D) should have chosen

12 Now that we are stuck in the elevator, I'm sure that the mechanic _____ it yesterday.

(A) must have no repaired

(B) must have not repaired

(C) didn't must have repaired

(D) doesn't must have repaired

Error Recognition

 틀린 문장 고르기

다음 중 문법적으로 <u>틀린</u> 것을 고르세요.

A teacher showed his students a dark, empty hall. "Buy something to fill this dark hall," he said. The teacher saw them ❶ look at it carefully. The first student filled the hall with expensive hay. The teacher said, "The hall is full, but even darker." The teacher had them ❷ to create a brighter atmosphere in the hall. The second student bought a cheap candle. The rest of the students helped her ❸ to put the candles in some kind of shape. The teacher ❹ noticed them trying to make a heart shape with the candles. Lighting the candle, the teacher told the students, "Well done! Now the hall is filled with light." One of the students said "Our class president's idea was great!" The teacher thought they ❺ might have planned to arrange something in a heart shape in the hall.

 고쳐쓰기

틀린 문장의 번호를 쓰고 올바르게 고치세요.

 틀린 문장 고르기

다음 중 문법적으로 <u>틀린</u> 것을 고르세요.

Betty thinks to herself that she can ① **reason** from anything like Sherlock Holmes, the famous detective. One day, a new family moved in next door. Betty was sure there was something ② **strange** about them. Then one day, her other neighbor, Minnie called. Her favorite vase was gone. Who took it? Betty decided to find the truth. Minnie told Betty she kept the vase under a window near the back door. Betty observed someone ③ **had left** a small footprint by the window near the back door. Betty looked ④ **even** more closely and she saw some mud on the floor. Right by the footprint there was some green paint on the floor. She remembered that her new neighbors were painting their fence green. She felt sure that her new neighbors ⑤ **could have taken** the vase. But early the next morning, Betty's phone rang. It was Minnie. She had found her vase. Her mother had used it to take some flowers to Minnie's grandmother in the hospital!

 고쳐쓰기

틀린 문장의 번호를 쓰고 올바르게 고치세요.

 _____

배운 내용 스스로 정리해보기

① 지각 · 사역동사

지각동사와 사역동사의 목적격 보어는 ❶ ⬚⬚⬚⬚⬚ 을(를) 쓴다. 지각동사가 올 때 목적어와

목적격 보어가 ❷ ⬚⬚⬚⬚ 관계면 목적격보어에 ❸ ⬚⬚⬚⬚ 또는 ❹ ⬚⬚⬚⬚⬚ 을(를)

쓸 수 있고, ❺ ⬚⬚⬚⬚ 이(가) 올 경우는 동작의 진행을 강조할 때 쓰인다.

예시문장 써보기

❶ 지각동사가 쓰인 문장 ➜ _____

❷ 사역동사가 쓰인 문장 ➜ _____

❸ 준사역동사가 쓰인 문장 ➜ _____

② 조동사

조동사는 ❶ ⬚⬚⬚⬚ 동사나 ❷ ⬚⬚⬚⬚⬚ 동사 앞에 쓰여서 그 동사에 어떤 특정한 의미를

부여하는 동사이다. 조동사 뒤에는 반드시 ❸ ⬚⬚⬚⬚ 즉 동사원형이 와야한다.

예시문장 써보기

❶ 조동사 may와 일반동사를 사용하여 영작

➜ _____

❷ 조동사 must를 사용하여 영작

➜ _____

❸ 조동사+have+p.p.를 사용하여 영작

➜ _____

UNIT 02

—

to부정사

개념	**'to + 동사원형'** ex) I love **to eat** dessert after dinner.
쓰임	**문장에서 동사가 아닌 다른 형태로 쓰일 필요가 있을 때** ① **명사:** 주어, 보어, 목적어 자리에 쓰임 ex)　주어 **To wash hands** is essential before eating. ② **형용사:** 명사를 수식하거나 보어자리에 쓰여 　　서술어 역할을 함 ex)　명사 수식 There are a lot of topics **to debate.** ③ **부사:** 형용사, 부사, 동사를 수식하는 역할을 함 ex)　목적 Anne studied **to pass the exam**.

UNIT 2 to부정사

① to부정사의 명사적 용법

to부정사는 1) 주어, 2) 보어, 3) 목적어 자리에 쓰여 명사로서의 역할을 한다.

주어	<u>To find</u> your dream is important. <u>How</u> <u>to persuade</u> parents is difficult. 의문사 + to부정사
보어	주격보어 His fault is <u>to break</u> the promise with his fans. 목적격보어 A cup of coffee enabled him <u>to wake</u> up.
목적어	I agreed <u>to go</u> on a date with her. I don't know <u>how</u> <u>to treat</u> the baby. 의문사 + to부정사

② to부정사의 형용사적 용법

to부정사는 1) 명사를 수식하는 형용사로서의 역할을 하며(한정적 용법), 2) 보어자리에 쓰여 서술어로서의 형용사 역할을 하기도 한다(서술적 용법).

한정적 용법	She has no one <u>to help her</u>. I have nothing <u>to eat</u>. Exercise is the best way <u>to lose weight</u>. be동사가 있는 경우 I <u>am</u> <u>to meet</u> him tomorrow. 관계대명사가 있는 경우 He has no house <u>to live</u> <u>in</u>. = He has no house <u>in which</u> <u>to live</u>. = He has no house <u>which</u> <u>to live</u> <u>in</u>.
서술적 용법	주격보어 She is said <u>to be</u> rich. 목적격보어 I guess him <u>to be</u> about 30 years old.

NOTE

TIP 가주어 it, 진주어 to부정사

- It is natural for you to get angry with him.
  (= It is natural that you should get angry with him.)

TIP 가목적어 it, 진목적어 to부정사

- He makes it a rule to take a walk every morning.

**TIP be to 용법
(be동사+to부정사)**

- (예정) I am to study tomorrow.
- (의무) She knows what is to be done.
- (목적, 의도) Work hard if you are to pass the exam.
- (가능) Happiness is not to be bought with money.
- (운명) He was to die young, leaving his wife and a son.

③ to부정사의 부사적 용법

to부정사는 형용사, 부사, 동사를 수식하는 부사로서의 역할을 하며, 1) 목적, 2) 결과, 3) 원인, 4) 이유 / 판단의 근거, 5) 조건 / 양보의 의미를 갖는다.

목적	He came **to meet** me. = He came <u>so as[in order]</u> **to meet** me. = He came <u>so that</u> he <u>might[could]</u> <u>meet</u> me.
결과	Messi <u>grew up</u> **to be** a great man. Kim studied hard <u>only</u> **to fail** the exam.
원인	I'm sorry **to hear** the bad news.
이유 판단	He must be a fool **to believe** Jessi.
조건 양보	<u>To hear</u> him talk, you <u>would</u> take him for an American.

NOTE

TIP 무의지 동사

● 'live, awake, grow up' 등 무의지 동사 다음에 나오는 to부정사는 결과적 의미임.

→ **too와 to부정사**

'too-to부정사'는 '너무 ~해서 (동사원형)할 수 없다'의 의미를 갖는다.

- Jack and Amy are <u>too</u> **old to work**.

= Jack and Amy are <u>so</u> <u>old</u> <u>that</u> they cannot work.

→ **enough와 to부정사**

'형용사/부사 + enough to 부정사'는 'to부정사하기에 충분히~하다'의 의미를 갖는다.

- I am **old** <u>enough</u> **to vote**.

= I am <u>so</u> <u>old</u> <u>that</u> I <u>can</u> vote.

TIP so 형용사/
부사 that 주어 + 동사

● 너무 ~해서 주어가 동사하다

Exercise

 ## Exercise 1

둘 중 맞는 단어를 골라 문장을 완성하세요.

1. **Spend / To spend** lots of time with family is a great thing.

2. My job is **manage / to manage** the schedule of the team members.

3. I wish **to study / studying** abroad in the near future.

4. Would you like something **drink / to drink** while waiting in line?

5. Objective attitude is important **to make / making** a calm judgement.

 ## Exercise 2

주어진 단어들을 바르게 배열해 문장을 완성하세요.

1. 솔직히 말하면, 나는 이 방을 지금 당장 나가고 싶다.

→ _____.

   (I, right now, this room, to be honest, to, want, leave)

2. 내 여동생은 훌륭한 바이올리니스트가 되기 위해 바이올린을 열심히 연주했다.

→ _____.

   (played the violin, a great violinist, my sister, to, hard, become)

3. Nina가 학급 회의를 놓친걸 보니 아픈 것 같다.

→ _____.

   (the class meeting, Nina, miss, to, be sick, may)

 ## Exercise 3

주어진 단어를 활용하여 빈칸을 채워 문장을 완성하세요.

---

❶ How _____ to the main office is explained on our website and map. (go)

❷ That idol group member is the one to lead her group and _____ a main dancer. (be)

❸ Customers told the manager _____ to them for staff's rude behavior. (apologize)

❹ His grandmother was surprised _____ her grandson got the highest score in his class. (hear)

❺ I would be happy _____ a gold medal for next competition. (receive)

❻ The group who supported the losing team was so _____ that they couldn't speak out anything in the interview. (disappoint)

Sentence Completion

1 _____ in front of everyone is a challenge for me.

(A) Speak

(B) Spoke

(C) Speaks

(D) To speak

4 She doesn't know what _____ now.

(A) did

(B) to do

(C) doing

(D) have done

2 _____ your dentist regularly for your teeth is important.

(A) Visit

(B) Visits

(C) Visited

(D) To visit

5 He invited everyone _____ to the party.

(A) come

(B) came

(C) to come

(D) have come

3 My goal is _____ all around Europe.

(A) travel

(B) traveled

(C) to travel

(D) have traveled

6 Our team is _____ for presentation next week.

(A) prepare

(B) to prepare

(C) to preparing

(D) have prepared

7 He doesn't have a private space

to take some rest.

(A) to

(B) in

(C) to which

(D) in which

8 That weather forecaster is said

the wrong information in a voice filled with conviction.

(A) to report

(B) to reported

(C) to reporting

(D) of reporting

9 She exercises every other day

healthy.

(A) stay

(B) to stay

(C) staying

(D) to staying

10 The girl is not tall   to ride the rollercoaster.

(A) so

(B) too

(C) enough

(D) in order

11 My friend is too   to take part in the basketball competition.

(A) tall

(B) taller

(C) small

(D) smaller

12 We   to reducing environmental pollution by using sustainable fabric in fashion design.

(A) decide

(B) contribute

(C) would decide

(D) would contribute

UNIT 2　to부정사

Error Recognition

● TOSEL 기출문제 변형 수능/내신 출제유형

 틀린 문장 고르기

다음 중 문법적으로 <u>틀린</u> 것을 고르세요.

The Great Morinda is a yellow fruit that ❶ **grows** in Australia, India, Vietnam, and some islands such as Hawaii. The Great Morinda has many names, but one of its popular names ❷ **is** the "Cheese Fruit." It is called this because it has a smell that is a lot like stinky cheese. The fruit smells because it needs ❸ **so attract** fruit bats. The bats eat the fruit, and then drop the seeds in different places. This helps the plant ❹ **grow** . The Great Morinda is very sour in taste. It is a good source of vitamin C. Many things are made from the fruit. It is used in several traditional medicines. It is used ❺ **to treat** back pain, knee problems, and fatigue. To become a medicine, the fruit is put in a powder or juice.

 고쳐쓰기

틀린 문장의 번호를 쓰고 올바르게 고치세요.

 ● TOSEL 기출문제 변형 수능/내신 출제유형

틀린 문항 고르기

다음 중 문법적으로 <u>틀린</u> 것을 고르세요.

Mandy really wanted a pet. She first thought it ① **was** be great to have a dog. She begged her parents for a puppy. But her parents said no. She was sad ② **to hear** she couldn't have a puppy. So she asked for a cat. Mandy's parents thought about it. Then finally they said it was okay ③ **to get** a cat. Mandy went to the local shelter. At the shelter there were lots of cats. She felt bad looking at all the cats. She could not choose just one! So instead, Mandy decided to become a volunteer. Her job was ④ **to take** care of all the cats. She liked most of her tasks. One task was to take pictures of the cats. Another task was to play with the cats. The least fun task was to clean the cage. But out of all of this, Mandy learned that you do not need to own a pet ⑤ **to spend** time with animals.

고쳐쓰기

틀린 문장의 번호를 쓰고 올바르게 고치세요.

⟶ _____

✏️ 배운 내용 스스로 정리해보기

① **to부정사의 명사적 용법**

부정사는 ❶ _____, ❷ _____, ❸ _____ 자리에 쓰여 명사로서의 역할을 한다.

예시문장 써보기

❶ 주어 ➡ _____

❷ 보어 ➡ _____

② **to부정사의 형용사적 용법**

부정사는 ❶ _____ 을(를) 수식하는 형용사로서의 역할을 하며(한정적 용법), ❷ _____

자리에 쓰여 서술어로서의 형용사 역할을 하기도 한다(서술적 용법).

예시문장 써보기

❶ 한정적 용법 ➡ _____

❷ 서술적 용법 ➡ _____

③ **to부정사의 부사적 용법**

부정사는 부사로서의 역할을 하며, ❶ _____, ❷ _____, ❸ _____

❹ 이유·판단의 근거, ❺ 조건·양보의 의미를 갖는다.

예시문장 써보기

❶ 목적 ➡ _____

❷ 결과 ➡ _____

UNIT 03

동명사

개념	동사원형 + -ing
	ex) __Being__ honest is always important.

쓰임	문장 속에서 주어·목적어·보어의 기능을 함
	❶ 주어
	ex) __Traveling__ Europe is one of my future plans.
	❷ 목적어
	ex) Do you mind __watching__ a comedy show?
	❸ 보어
	ex) His hobby is __writing__ letters.

❶ 동명사의 기능

동명사의 품사는 **명사로 ~하는 것, ~하기**로 해석되며, 문장 속에서 **주어·목적어·보어**의 기능을 한다.

주어	<u>Watching</u> movies encourages creative ideas. = <u>It</u> encourages creative ideas <u>watching</u> movies. 가주어 진주어
보어	주격보어 Her job is <u>selling</u> cars.
목적어	타동사의 목적어 That woman enjoys <u>chattering</u>. 전치사의 목적어 I am sure of Jason's <u>succeeding</u>.
동격	His research, <u>investigating</u> the virus, is interesting.

➡ **동명사의 관용 표현**

　'feel like + 동명사'는 '(동명사)하고 싶다'의 의미를 갖는다.
　'be busy + 동명사'는 '(동명사)하느라 바쁘다'의 의미를 갖는다.

- I don't feel much like **<u>working</u>** today.

- I'm busy **<u>studying</u>** two foreign languages.

❷ 행위명사

동명사가 **관사 · 소유격 · 형용사** 다음에 온 경우, **주어 · 목적어 · 보어**를 취할 수 없다.

> - The team has gone into a hard <u>training</u>.
>
> - Early <u>rising</u> might not always be the short-cut to success.
>
> - I've conducted my research, analyzed my <u>findings</u> and written my results.
>
> - I don't want to be known just for my look and my <u>dancing</u>.

NOTE ✏

TIP

● 행위명사에서 동명사는 명사의 기능만을 하며 복수형이 가능하다.

UNIT 3 행위명사

Exercise

 ## Exercise 1

둘 중 맞는 단어를 골라 문장을 완성하세요.

❶ **Drink / Drinking** too much coffee can make you anxious.

❷ Jason doesn't feel like **work / working** out after work today.

❸ It is exciting **solving / solved** difficult problems in the math class.

❹ Prevention of epidemics is **utilization / utilizing** advanced technology.

❺ Those students enjoy **doing / to do** lots of activities during classes.

 ## Exercise 2

주어진 단어들을 바르게 배열해 문장을 완성하세요.

❶ 다양한 경험을 하는 것은 직업을 고르는데 영향을 미친다.

→ _____.

   (occupation, experience, an, having, diverse, affects, choosing)

❷ 내가 해야 하는 일은 우리의 계획을 위해 뒤섞인 목록들을 재배열하는 것이다.

→ _____.

   (scrambled, for our project, I have to do, rearranging, what, lists, is)

❸ 그들은 전례없는 도전을 수행하는 것을 두려워하지 않는다.

→ _____.

   (aren't, they, afraid of, carrying out, unprecedented challenges, the)

 Exercise 3

주어진 단어를 활용하여 빈칸을 채워 문장을 완성하세요.

1 Mike's hobby is _____ the model of Saturn V rocket ships. (collect)

2 Some intelligent engineers consider _____ in Silicon Valley. (work)

3 I was busy _____ for the upcoming exams. (prepare)

4 Having a habit of _____ regularly is important for writers. (write)

5 My senior is in charge of the main project, _____ the number of criminals. (investigate)

6 His _____ is affected by Martin Ramirez's artwork. (draw)

Sentence Completion

① _____ for the correct information on the internet is important.

(A) Search
(B) Searched
(C) Searching
(D) In searching

④ Hong Kong culture of _____ hot tea relieves abdominal pain.

(A) drunk
(B) drinks
(C) drinking
(D) will drink

② It is valuable for next year's plan _____ back on the last year.

(A) looked
(B) looking
(C) by looking
(D) have looked

⑤ The person who doesn't have a firm motivation gives up _____ patient with the difficulties.

(A) is
(B) are
(C) being
(D) will be

③ One of the ways anthropologists investigate other cultures is _____ with the locals.

(A) live
(B) lived
(C) living
(D) have lived

⑥ My older brother minds _____ the music while studying.

(A) turns on
(B) to turn on
(C) turning on
(D) of turning on

7 All the kids in the town enjoy
_____ in that park.

(A) play
(B) played
(C) to play
(D) playing

8 We can play soccer instead of
_____ books during our break
time.

(A) read
(B) reading
(C) to read
(D) to reading

9 One of the easiest ways for completing
tasks _____ combining the
previous data.

(A) is
(B) are
(C) to be
(D) being

10 The event organizer is working on the
_____ of bountiful events.

(A) to plan
(B) planned
(C) planning
(D) have planned

11 Presidential election is set for Autumn
2021, and the region's _____
is due in Spring 2022.

(A) vote
(B) voting
(C) will vote
(D) will be voting

12 Our classmates' habit, _____
on a daily basis, led to improved scores
on exams.

(A) study
(B) studies
(C) studying
(D) have studied

Error Recognition

 틀린 문장 고르기

다음 중 문법적으로 <u>틀린</u> 것을 고르세요.

Every year there is a parade in Masaba City for ❶ celebrating the city's anniversary. This year, the theme of the parade was "gardens." The parade had musicians and dancers. But best of all ❷ were the floats-big platforms carried on top of cars. One float was shaped like a vegetable garden. The people on the platform were dressed ❸ as carrots, tomatoes, spinach, pumpkins, and eggplants. Around them there were big fake ❹ plants decorated in sparkly green material. Another float was decorated like a big flower garden. On that float, the mayor of the city and his wife and children sat waving at the crowd. They were intent on ❺ take charge of the bright atmosphere.

 고쳐쓰기

틀린 문장의 번호를 쓰고 올바르게 고치세요.

→ _____

 틀린 문장 고르기

다음 중 문법적으로 <u>틀린</u> 것을 고르세요.

Today, my father and mother surprised me at my after-school drama class. At four o'clock, they came and picked ❶ **me up** . I asked them why they came, but they would not tell me. First, we went home. They told me ❷ **to change** into my best dress. Then, my mom styled my hair. Finally, we all got into the car. I asked again, and this time they told me we were going to a musical! My parents and I arrived ❸ **at** the theater. We watched a wonderful play. The actors sang and danced to beautiful music. When the musical finished, we went to the front lobby. There, I talked to all of the actors and ❹ **took** a picture with them. I thanked my parents for ❺ **gave** me a fun surprise after school!

 고쳐쓰기

틀린 문장의 번호를 쓰고 올바르게 고치세요.

 배운 내용 스스로 정리해보기

① 동명사의 기능

동명사의 품사는 ❶ [ ] (으)로 ~하는 것, ~하기로 해석되며, 문장 속에서 ❷ [ ], ❸ [ ], ❹ [ ] 의 기능을 한다.

예시문장 써보기

❶ 주어 → _____

❷ 목적어 → _____

❸ 보어 → _____

② 행위명사

동명사가 ❶ [ ], ❷ [ ], ❸ [ ] 다음에 온 경우, ❹ [ ], ❺ [ ], ❻ [ ] 을(를) 취할 수 없다.

예시문장 써보기

❶ the와 행위명사를 사용해 영작

→ _____

❷ new와 행위명사를 사용해 영작

→ _____

UNIT 04

to부정사구와 동명사구

생김새	① **to부정사: 'to + 동사원형'** ex) It's an honor **to lead** our team. ② **동명사: '동사원형 + -ing'** ex) **Learning** foreign languages is quite difficult.
비교	① **to부정사의 의미상 주어: 'for + 목적격' 또는 'of + 목적격'** ② **동명사의 의미상 주어: 소유격** ③ **to부정사 / 동명사를 목적어로 취하는 동사** ex) to부정사만: He pretends **to do** his homework. 동명사만: I advocate **protecting** the environment. **to부정사와 동명사를 모두 목적어로 취하는 동사** ex) I forgot **to close** the door. ex) I forgot **closing** the door.

UNIT ④ to부정사구와 동명사구

❶ 의미상 주어

1. 의미상 주어의 생략

> ### ❶ 주절의 주어와 같을 때
>
> `to 부정사` I wish **to call** on you on Saturday.
>
> `동명사` He succeeded in **passing** the examination.
>
> ### ❷ 일반인(people, you, they, etc.)일 때
>
> `to 부정사` It is not desirable **to tell** a lie.
>
> `동명사` **Eating** too much is not good for health.

2. to 부정사의 의미상 주어

for + 목적격	It is difficult <u>for</u> **me** <u>to lift</u> a big stone.
of + 목적격	It is kind <u>of</u> **you** <u>to lend</u> your blanket.

3. 동명사의 의미상 주어

소유격	Bella doesn't like <u>his</u> **going** to the party.

❷ to부정사·동명사의 시제

단순	`to부정사` He thinks Milla to be honest. = He thinks that Milla is honest.
	`동명사` She is proud of her husband being famous. = She is proud that her husband is famous.
완료	`to부정사` He regrets to have spent too much money. = He regrets that he spent too much money.
	`동명사` I am ashamed of having been idle. = I am ashamed that I was idle.

TIP of + 목적격을 사용하는 경우

● 사람을 주어로 취하여 사람의 행동이나 성질에 대한 판단을 나타낼 때 씀.

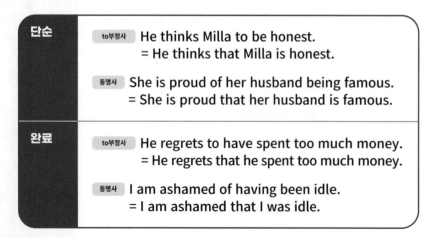

clever	영리한
foolish	어리석은
generous	관대한
good	친절한
mean	야비한
naughty	못된, 버릇없는
impudent	무례한
spiteful	심술궂은
wicked	사악한

❸ to부정사·동명사를 목적어로 쓰는 동사

to부정사 또는 동명사만을 목적어로 취하는 동사가 있다.

> **to 부정사** He wants <u>to watch</u> a German movie.
>
> **동명사** He enjoys <u>watching</u> German movies.

→ to부정사와 동명사를 모두 목적어로 쓰는 동사

to부정사와 동명사 중 무엇을 목적어로 취하는지에 따라 의미가 변화하는 동사들이 있다.

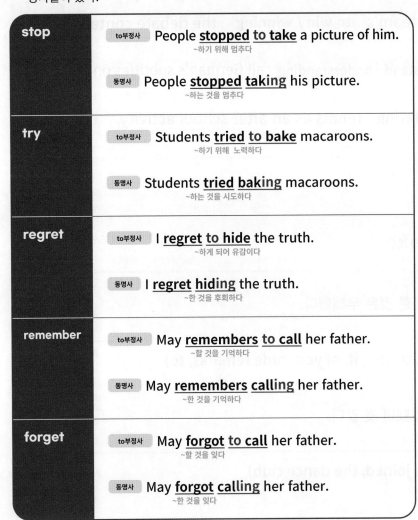

stop	**to부정사** People <u>stopped to take</u> a picture of him. ~하기 위해 멈추다
	동명사 People <u>stopped taking</u> his picture. ~하는 것을 멈추다
try	**to부정사** Students <u>tried to bake</u> macaroons. ~하기 위해 노력하다
	동명사 Students <u>tried baking</u> macaroons. ~하는 것을 시도하다
regret	**to부정사** I <u>regret to hide</u> the truth. ~하게 되어 유감이다
	동명사 I <u>regret hiding</u> the truth. ~한 것을 후회하다
remember	**to부정사** May <u>remembers to call</u> her father. ~할 것을 기억하다
	동명사 May <u>remembers calling</u> her father. ~한 것을 기억하다
forget	**to부정사** May <u>forgot to call</u> her father. ~할 것을 잊다
	동명사 May <u>forgot calling</u> her father. ~한 것을 잊다

NOTE ✎

TIP to부정사만을 목적어로 쓰는 동사

ask	요구하다
wish	바라다 [희망하다]
desire	
want	
decide	결정하다
refuse	거절하다
plan	계획하다
resolve	해결하다
promise	약속하다
prepare	준비하다
enable	가능하게 하다
pretend	…인 척하다

TIP 동명사만을 목적어로 쓰는 동사

allow	허락하다
avoid	피하다
mind	꺼리다
give up	포기하다
finish	끝내다
admit	인정하다
involve	포함하다
suggest	제안하다
advocate	지지하다
deny	부인하다
resist	저항하다
enjoy	즐기다

TIP used to

used to 부정사	~하곤 했다
be used to 부정사	사용되다
be used to -ing	~하는 데에 익숙하다

TIP to부정사와 동명사를 모두
목적어로 쓰는 동사(의미 동일)

begin	시작하다
like	좋아하다
start	시작하다
continue	계속하다
hate	싫어하다

Exercise

 ### Exercise 1

둘 중 맞는 단어를 고르세요.

1. **Roll / Rolling** the eyes sometimes helps to recover the vision.

2. It is easy **for him / of him** to complete the most difficult task.

3. I support **for my friend / my friend's** preparing for the exhibition.

4. They are sure of our team's **to win / winning** the debate contest.

5. He pretends **to understand / understanding** all German's subtitles on the video.

6. We enjoy **to play / playing** tennis as an after school activity.

 ### Exercise 2

주어진 단어들을 바르게 배열하세요.

1. 네가 그에게 무례한 말을 한 것은 무례했다.

   ➜ _____.

   (was impudent, make, to him, it, of you, rude remarks, to)

2. Luca는 춤 동아리에 가입했던 것 같다.

   ➜ _____.

   (to, Luca, have, seems, joined, the dance club)

3. 학급 회장은 반대 의견을 수용하려고 노력하는 중이다.

   ➜ _____.

   (to, the class president, trying, is, opposite views, accommodate)

 Exercise 3

괄호 안의 표현을 알맞은 형태로 빈칸에 쓰세요.

① Some children promised _____ higher scores on the following English test. (get)

② It is quite common _____ to battle vocal cord nodules. (singers)

③ My teacher likes _____ being able to transfer to the new school. (her student)

④ He is proud of _____ the tricky inspection at the border. (pass)

⑤ Our human resources team considers this patissier _____ appropriate for our position. (be)

⑥ The girl finished _____ the journal article for the upcoming festival. (edit)

Sentence Completion

① It should be banned ⬚⬚⬚⬚⬚⬚ a car without a driving license.

(A) drive

(B) drove

(C) to drive

(D) to driving

② He continues ⬚⬚⬚⬚⬚ the problem in many ways to become a renowned scientist.

(A) solving

(B) his solving

(C) her solving

(D) their solving

③ It is clever ⬚⬚⬚⬚⬚ to get out of the pitfall without any difficulties.

(A) him

(B) of him

(C) for him

(D) that he

④ This bike infrastructure was built ⬚⬚⬚⬚⬚⬚ to ride the bike to avoid traffic.

(A) work

(B) workers

(C) for workers

(D) for working

⑤ Advertisers order influencers' putting on the advertising products regularly and ⬚⬚⬚⬚⬚ about them on their channel.

(A) mentioning

(B) mentioned

(C) to mention

(D) to mentioning

⑥ Due to the advent of AI technologies, we are worried about many jobs' ⬚⬚⬚⬚⬚ .

(A) disappear

(B) disappears

(C) to disappear

(D) disappearing

7 The previous tenant seemed

⬛⬛⬛⬛⬛ the house without

asking the landlord's permission.

(A) renovate

(B) renovating

(C) to have renovated

(D) to having renovated

8 Lots of participants in this choir feel

satisfied with ⬛⬛⬛⬛⬛ for the

national singing competition.

(A) apply

(B) applied

(C) have applied

(D) having applied

9 Dr. Whang said the newly found method

would enable ⬛⬛⬛⬛⬛ hydrogen

as an alternative energy source.

(A) using

(B) to use

(C) to using

(D) of using

10 The person who easily gives up anything

avoids ⬛⬛⬛⬛⬛

the unexperienced things.

(A) challenge

(B) challenging

(C) to challenge

(D) to challenging

11 A new accountant regrets

⬛⬛⬛⬛⬛ her customer's call

while working on the project.

(A) to miss

(B) missing

(C) have missed

(D) to having missed

12 You should try ⬛⬛⬛⬛⬛

the cookies for trial before presenting

them to your customers.

(A) to bake

(B) baking

(C) of baking

(D) by baking

UNIT 4 to부정사구와 동명사구

Error Recognition

● TOSEL 기출문제 변형 수능/내신 출제유형

 틀린 문장 고르기

다음 중 문법적으로 <u>틀린</u> 것을 고르세요.

Yesterday, Leila's class did an interesting activity. They called it "panning" for gold. First, the students planned **① going** to a small river. Near the river, they shovelled dirt into pans. Then, they added water from the river **② to** the pan, little by little. They moved the dirt around in the water. Gold is **③ heavier** than small rocks and sand, so it stayed in the bottom of the pan. That way, Leila and the other students could keep gold on one side and let the water, sand, and rocks out the other side. Leila found a very small bit of gold. She is going to use the gold to make her mom some earrings. Therefore, she put the gold in a little plastic container **④ to take** home. Teacher is proud of **⑤ her getting** a gold even if it's not a lot.

 고쳐쓰기

틀린 문장의 번호를 쓰고 올바르게 고치세요.

⟶ _____

 틀린 문장 고르기

다음 중 문법적으로 <u>틀린</u> 것을 고르세요.

How many mammals can fly? At first, it may seem there **❶ are** many flying mammals. Opossums, for example, are famous for moving in the air between tree branches. However, this is not flying. It is only gliding. It is common **❷ of opossums** to use the wind and their feather-like tail to move. Another similar mammal is the flying squirrel. Flying squirrels do not really fly at all. Instead, they jump really far. They stretch their furry skin when they want **❸ to go** long distances. It seems to enable the squirrels **❹ to fly**, but they are just gliding. In fact, the only truly flying mammals are bats. Bats are mammals that use their wings for powered flight. And there are a lot of bats. Almost 20% of all species of mammals **❺ are** bats. Therefore, many mammals can fly, but only if they are bats.

 고쳐쓰기

틀린 문장의 번호를 쓰고 올바르게 고치세요.

_____

✏️ 배운 내용 스스로 정리해보기

① <u>의미상 주어</u>

문장의 주어와 to부정사 또는 동명사의 주어가 다른 경우 의미상 주어를 쓰고, to부정사는

❶ _____, ❷ _____, 동명사는 ❸ _____ (으)로 나타낸다.

예시문장 써보기

❶ for + 목적격 ➜ _____

❷ of + 목적격 ➜ _____

❸ 소유격 ➜ _____

② <u>to부정사·동명사의 시제</u>

to부정사나 동명사의 시제가 본동사보다 더 이전에 일어난 일을 나타낼 때 to부정사는

❶ _____, 동명사는 ❷ _____ (으)로 나타낸다.

예시문장 써보기

❶ to + have + 과거분사

➜ _____

❷ having + 과거분사

➜ _____

③ <u>to부정사·동명사를 목적어로 쓰는 동사</u>

❶ _____ 또는 ❷ _____ 만을 목적어로 취하는 동사들이 있다.

예시문장 써보기

❶ to부정사만 목적어가 되는 문장

➜ _____

❷ 동명사만 목적어가 되는 문장

➜ _____

TOSEL 실전문제 ②

PART 6. Sentence Completion

DIRECTIONS: In this portion of the test, you will be given 12 incomplete sentences. From the choices provided, choose the word or words that correctly complete the sentence. Then, fill in the corresponding space on your answer sheet.

1. I believe friends should _____ each other's confidence and not share other's secrets.

   (A) keep
   (B) kept
   (C) keeps
   (D) be kept

2. I felt my palms _____ whenever I get so nervous or too stressed out.

   (A) sweat
   (B) sweated
   (C) to sweat
   (D) to get sweat

3. BT & B telecommunications company has decided to reduce its rates as a way of _____ more customers.

   (A) attract
   (B) attracting
   (C) attractive
   (D) to attract

4. _____ fine furniture, Jerome's Furniture uses special wood that is not available in stores.

   (A) Build
   (B) Built
   (C) To build
   (D) Have built

5. It is very kind _____ to come all the way to the airport to meet me.

   (A) you
   (B) of you
   (C) for you
   (D) that you

6. The geometry question number 10 was too _____ to even try to solve it.

   (A) tougher
   (B) difficult
   (C) the toughest
   (D) more difficult

7. The regulations indicate that calculators _____ not be used during the examination.

(A) may
(B) need
(C) had better
(D) would like to

10. _____ a famous star is a difficult goal for most actors to achieve.

(A) Become
(B) Becomes
(C) Becoming
(D) Had become

8. The purpose of today's meeting _____ a successor to the president of the student council.

(A) choose
(B) choosing
(C) had chosen
(D) is to choose

11. My parents enjoy _____ a walk in the park after having dinner.

(A) take
(B) taking
(C) to take
(D) having taken

9. The _____ of agricultural products and seeds is prohibited in most countries.

(A) take
(B) taken
(C) taking
(D) to take

12. Ms. Howard received an award for _____ a new and innovative teaching-learning material.

(A) develop
(B) to develop
(C) have developed
(D) having developed

Error Recognition

 (1~2) 다음 중 문법적으로 틀린 것을 골라 고치세요.

1

One of the world's largest camera companies got its name in an **❶** interesting way. The head of the company, George Eastman, wanted a name that was short, easy **❷** to say , and different from any other company names. Most importantly, he wanted it **❸** include his favorite letter: K. After working with his mother for four years **❹** to think of the perfect name, they finally found it in 1888. That is how the Kodak Company was born, and it **❺** is still a leader in photos and printing today.

2

You may **1** have get some interesting gifts for your birthday, but one year Calvin Coolidge, the President of America, got the strangest gift of all. His friend Harvey Firestone was **2** very rich from selling car tires. He wanted **3** to give Coolidge a special gift, so he gave him a baby hippo! The President named **4** him Billy, and he lived longer than his owner! By the time Billy died, he had 23 children, and many of the hippos in American zoos today **5** are his grandchildren.

Error Recognition

 (3~6) 다음 중 문법적으로 틀린 것을 고르세요.

● TOSEL 기출문제 변형 수능/내신 출제유형

3

The White House is one of the most famous buildings in America, but it did not ❶ **always** have that name. The first stone was laid in 1792, but it took eight years ❷ **of it** to build. When President John Adams moved in in 1800, it ❸ **was called** "The President's Palace." Later, it was known as "The Executive Mansion." In 1901, President Roosevelt began ❹ **to remodel** the building. After that, he changed the name ❺ **to** "The White House." That's the name it has had ever since.

● TOSEL 기출문제 변형 수능/내신 출제유형

4

Nowadays, armies fight each other from a distance with missiles and airplanes, ❶ **but** this is not a new idea. More than 700 years ago, the Chinese army was ❷ **doing** the same thing, only with birds. They would ❸ **tie** hot rocks around the necks of birds and send them into enemy's cities to set everything on fire from a distance. The birds were difficult ❹ **to control** , however, and the Chinese army started ❺ **used** paper rockets that were shaped like birds instead. This was centuries before missiles became common in war.

5

Around Christmas time, it can be expensive ❶ **to give** gifts to all of your friends or coworkers. In America, there are special ways of ❷ **to get** around this problem. One of the most popular of these is Secret Santa, where each person ❸ **secretly** gives a gift to only one other person. Another custom is a White Elephant Party, where each person ❹ **gives** a gift from their own house that they don't need anymore. Other options include the Pollyanna Swap and Cobweb Party. Maybe you can ❺ **try** one of these tricks next time when Christmas comes around.

6

As humans get older, they tend ❶ **slowing** down, until eventually they just stop. Most animals do the same thing, but some animals don't seem to get older at all. Lobsters, turtles, and clams ❷ **are** among the animals that don't die from old age. One clam was found ❸ **to be** over 500 years old. These animals only die from diseases or accidents or ❹ **being** eaten by a human. Glass sponges are the champions, though, because they seem ❺ **to live** for over 10,000 years.

수능 대비 문제

CHAPTER 03

III. 분사

UNIT 01

현재분사

생김새	**동사 + ing** ex) I saw the man (who was) <u>**walking**</u> along the coast.
쓰임	**동사의 형태를 변형시켜 명사를 수식하거나** **주격 보어·목적격 보어로 쓸 때 능동·진행·상태의 의미를 가짐** **❶ 명사 수식** ex) The man <u>**speaking**</u> French is my father-in-law. **❷ 주격 보어** ex) The game looks <u>**interesting**</u>. **❸ 목적격 보어** ex) I saw the baby (who was) <u>**crying**</u> on the sofa.

❶ 능동의 의미

분사와 수식을 받는 명사의 의미상 관계가 **능동**인 경우 현재분사를 쓴다.

> There is a **sleep**ing dog in the garden.
>
> We can buy a magazine **contain**ing the news for a dollar.
>
> The boys **play**ing soccer are my friends.
>
> Look at the **ris**ing sun in the sky.

➡ **유사분사**

관계대명사로 문장을 전환할 때 능동태로 쓰이는 동사의 분사형이다.

> • They are the English-**speak**ing people.
> = They are the people who **speak** English.
>
> • She wears the tight-**fit**ting shoes.
> = She wears the shoes which **fit** tight.
>
> • A handsome-**look**ing boy is swimming in the pool.
> = A boy who **looks** handsome is swimming in the pool.
>
> • You should see a doctor before taking pain-**reliev**ing drugs.
> = You should see a doctor before taking drugs which **relieve** pain.

❷ 진행의 의미

분사와 수식을 받는 명사의 의미상 관계가 **진행**인 경우 현재분사를 쓴다.

> The girl (who is) **read**ing a newspaper is my cousin sister.
>
> I watched her **draw**ing a picture.

NOTE 🖊

TIP 관계대명사 생략

● '주격 관계대명사 + be동사'는 생략 가능함.

❸ 상태의 의미

분사와 수식을 받는 명사의 의미상 관계가 **상태**인 경우 현재분사를 쓴다.

> He was **sitting** in a restaurant at seven o'clock.
>
> The book **belonging** to this library was lost last night.
>
> She is **wearing** a pink dress today.

❹ 현재분사의 용법

한정용법: 분사가 수식을 받는 명사의 의미를 한정시키는 것
서술용법: 분사가 수식을 받는 명사의 의미를 더 자세히 풀어주는 것

한정용법	They were surprised by the **approaching** train.
	It is a **disappointing** result.
	The hen **making** strange noises is hers.
	Don't disturb the man **remaining** calm.
서술용법	주격보어 He sat **reading** a newspaper.
	Ann walked **eating** a sandwich.
	목적격보어 I saw her **running** across the street.
	I want her **attending** the party.

Exercise

 ## Exercise 1

둘 중 맞는 단어를 골라 문장을 완성하세요.

❶ The motorcycle stand / standing beside the bench is expensive.

❷ Some fresh-looking / looking-fresh vegetables are being sold.

❸ The students are playing / playing soccer in the red uniform are the ones who won the game.

❹ The child dance / dancing happily is my daughter.

❺ What they overlooked turned out to be an astonishing / astonished result.

 ## Exercise 2

주어진 단어들을 바르게 배열해 문장을 완성하세요.

❶ 울고 있는 그 아기는 Jenny의 여동생이다.

➜ _____.

(crying, is, Jenny's younger sister, the baby)

❷ 너는 정치적 이슈를 포함하고 있는 영화를 봐도 된다.

➜ _____.

(political issues, you, allowed to watch, are, containing, movies)

❸ 그들은 Kim이 만든 반짝이는 옷들을 입고 있다.

➜ _____?

(Kim made, are wearing, sparkling, they, which, clothes)

 ## Exercise 3

주어진 단어를 활용하여 빈칸을 채워 문장을 완성하세요.

1. Ariel found a _____ hermit crab when she reached the uninhabited island. (sing)

2. You have to pay attention to the _____ question which will decide whether you could pass or not. (follow)

3. Agatha knows that the boy _____ near the market has lost his mother. (sob)

4. While _____ a taxi, they discussed the problem of climate change. (take)

5. You will miss your family _____ good times you spent with them. (remember)

6. They are preparing for the assignment _____ the math problems. (solve)

Sentence Completion

1 She bought her husband a knitting kit _____ the manual since he required her to do so.

(A) including
(B) includes
(C) included
(D) to include

2 The man with a long beard _____ along the street got arrested on the charge of pickpocketing.

(A) walk
(B) walked
(C) walking
(D) was walking

3 Jason insisted that he had baked an enormous elephant- _____ cake for his neighbors.

(A) seen
(B) seeing
(C) looked
(D) looking

4 That bus which is _____ to the bus stop now is heading to the baseball stadium.

(A) approach
(B) approaches
(C) approached
(D) approaching

5 I met a _____ boy when I went to the hospital last week, and now I think I got a cold.

(A) cough
(B) coughs
(C) coughed
(D) coughing

6 That man _____ at the woman over there seems to be uneducated to ignore people around.

(A) shouting
(B) shouted
(C) for shout
(D) will shout

7 Since snakes were _____ when we visited the zoo, we couldn't see them.

(A) hibernate

(B) hibernated

(C) hibernating

(D) had hibernated

8 The dog _____ a yellow clothes is a guide dog which can go into the National Assembly building.

(A) fit

(B) fitted

(C) wears

(D) wearing

9 The tall man _____ on a tree really resembles my favorite actor, Park.

(A) leaning

(B) leaned

(C) to lean

(D) for lean

10 It is an honor to receive such a _____ Siberian tiger from the President.

(A) fascinate

(B) fascinates

(C) fascinated

(D) fascinating

11 I don't remember whether or not I turned off the heater before _____ the house.

(A) left

(B) leaving

(C) to leave

(D) will leave

12 Dali grew up in a rich family, and he created paintings he wanted not _____ about money.

(A) concern

(B) concerns

(C) of concern

(D) concerning

UNIT 1 현재분사

Error Recognition

 틀린 문장 고르기

다음 중 문법적으로 <u>틀린</u> 것을 고르세요.

The soup that Uncle Sam **①** makes is like no other soup. It is even better than Grandma's soup. It is somehow perfectly sweet, sour, and spicy all at the same time. It contains **②** stir-fried boneless chicken, fresh white mushrooms, red curry paste, diced onions, fish sauce, lime juice, chicken soup, and coconut milk. Uncle Sam **③** knowing that I like it really spicy, so when I visit, he adds extra curry paste and one chili pepper. When he **④** serves the soup, he puts chopped fresh cilantro on the top. Cilantro is an herb with a strong smell. My older sister hates the smell and taste of cilantro. But I love it, so I **⑤** put extra cilantro on mine. Uncle Sam also puts out a dish of lime wedges. We squeeze the limes on top of the soup.

 고쳐쓰기

틀린 문장의 번호를 쓰고 올바르게 고치세요.

 틀린 문장 고르기

다음 중 문법적으로 <u>틀린</u> 것을 고르세요.

Tamara was **①** going to be in a magic competition. She was a new magician. However, she had a great trick of her own. The trick **②** involving cards. This trick went like this: First, give the cards to an audience member. Then, tell that person to choose one card. After that, tell the audience member to **③** remember the card. Next, have the audience member shuffle the cards. Finally, find the person's card and ask "Is this yours?" Tamara was really good at the card trick. She had **④** practiced it with her family and friends. She thought she could win the competition. The competition was going to be on the stage at the theater downtown. Tamara rode her bike to the theater one hour before the competition. But when she **⑤** got to the theater it was dark. Tamara then realized it was the wrong day!

 고쳐쓰기

틀린 문장의 번호를 쓰고 올바르게 고치세요.

 _____

배운 내용 스스로 정리해보기

① 능동의 의미

분사와 수식을 받는 명사의 의미상 관계가 능동이면   을(를) 쓴다.

예시문장 써보기

➔ _____ (employee, distribute)

② 진행의 의미

분사와 수식을 받는 명사의 의미상 관계가 진행이면   을(를) 쓴다.

예시문장 써보기

➔ _____ (man, run)

③ 상태의 의미

분사와 수식을 받는 명사의 의미상 관계가 상태이면   을(를) 쓴다.

예시문장 써보기

➔ _____ (astronaut, wear)

④ 현재분사의 용법

분사가 수식을 받는 명사의 의미를 한정시키는 것을 ❶   이라고 하고,

더 자세히 의미를 풀어주는 것을 ❷   이라고 한다.

예시문장 써보기

❶ 한정용법

➔ _____

❷ 서술용법

➔ _____

UNIT 02

과거분사

생김새	**(규칙) 동사원형 + (e)d** ex) A lot of **touch<u>ed</u>** <u>people</u> took handkerchiefs out.
쓰임	**동사의 형태를 변형시켜 명사를 수식하거나** **주격 보어·목적격 보어로 쓸 때 수동·완료의 의미를 가짐** **❶ 명사 수식** 　ex) We tried to figure out the <u>unsolved</u> <u>problem</u>. **❷ 주격 보어** 　ex) <u>I</u> am **surprised** at your extensive knowledge. **❸ 목적격 보어** 　ex) I saw <u>the window</u> **<u>broken</u>**.

UNIT ② 과거분사

❶ 수동의 의미

분사와 수식을 받는 명사의 의미상 관계가 **수동**인 경우 과거분사를 쓴다.

> Money **lent** is money **spent**.
>
> There is a **broken** window in the house.

NOTE ✏

→ **유사분사**

관계대명사로 문장을 전환할 때 수동태로 쓰이는 동사의 분사형이다.

> • That is a horse-**drawn** cart.
> = That is a cart which is drawn by a horse.
>
> • They live in a money-**dominated** society.
> = They live in a society which is dominated by money.
>
> • She is a well-**known** pianist.
> = She is a pianist who is well **known** (to the world).
>
> • He lives in an ivy-**covered** house.
> = He lives in a house which is covered with ivy.

❷ 완료된 동작의 상태나 성질

분사와 수식을 받는 명사의 의미상 관계가 **완료**의 의미인 경우 과거분사를 쓴다.

> Be careful not to eat those **rotten** eggs.
>
> The police is struggling to catch an **escaped** convict.

③ 과거분사의 용법

한정용법: 분사가 수식을 받는 명사의 의미를 한정시키는 것
서술용법: 분사가 수식을 받는 명사의 의미를 더 자세히 풀어주는 것

한정용법	I have an **expired** ticket to the opera. This is a story **written** by a nine-year-old girl.
서술용법	주격보어 She felt **exhausted** after a hard work. He sat **surrounded** by his men. 목적격보어 I had my hair cut. I want the skirt **shortened**.

④ 감정동사

현재분사 The game was very **amusing**.

과거분사 We were **amused** over the game.

단어	뜻	단어	뜻
amaze	놀라게 하다	excite	흥분시키다
astonish		frighten	겁먹게 만들다
confuse	혼란스럽게 만들다	irritate	짜증나게 하다
delight	많은 기쁨을 주다	please	기쁘게 하다
disappoint	실망시키다	satisfy	만족시키다
embarrass	당황스럽게 만들다	surprise	놀라게 하다

UNIT 2 과거분사

Exercise

 ## Exercise 1

둘 중 맞는 단어를 골라 문장을 완성하세요.

❶ This wall is **coloring / colored** by a famous artist.

❷ Automatic doors **open / opening** by itself without an attempt to opening the door.

❸ The **motivated-well / well-motivated** man can succeed.

❹ None of them knew that he was **going / gone** .

❺ Nori was **frighten / frightened** by the storm.

 ## Exercise 2

주어진 단어들을 바르게 배열해 문장을 완성하세요.

❶ 내가 그녀를 찾았을 때, 그녀는 이미 경찰에게 잡혀있었다.

→ _____ .

(by the police, when, caught, I found, she was already, her)

❷ 학생들은 오늘 점심메뉴에 만족했다.

→ _____ .

(satisfied with, the students, lunch menu today, were, their)

❸ Greg는 그의 아버지에 의해 만들어진 정장을 입고 있다.

→ _____ .

(is wearing, Greg, is made, by his father, a suit which)

 ## Exercise 3

주어진 단어를 활용하여 빈칸을 채워 문장을 완성하세요.

❶ We went to see the _____ turtle down by the harbour. (capture)

❷ The show will start at 8 o'clock with _____ chimpanzees on the stage. (sing)

❸ Although there might be some difficulties, it is worth accepting _____ challenges. (expose)

❹ Lena wanted her hair _____ when she was young, but now she doesn't. (perm)

❺ The local residents were _____ by the construction site noise. (irritate)

❻ Her performance was _____ enough to make audiences applaud. (surprise)

Sentence Completion

1 The previous lecture he did was about saving the .... species all around the world.

(A) danger

(B) endanger

(C) dangerous

(D) endangered

2 The one who thinks that he could do anything is a .... person to succeed.

(A) prepare

(B) prepares

(C) prepared

(D) preparing

3 She takes a bus to her school every morning, which is .... by her grandfather.

(A) drive

(B) drove

(C) driven

(D) driving

4 Yesterday we chased the brown .... cat that lives in the school.

(A) dot

(B) dots

(C) doting

(D) dotted

5 .... vinyl is in fact reusable if it is cleaned and sorted when you discard it.

(A) Use

(B) Used

(C) Using

(D) Useful

6 Though the .... swelling was not deadly, it was in the part of the brain that is used when people listen to and make music.

(A) increase

(B) increased

(C) increasing

(D) increasingly

7 The _____ wall is dangerous, so we must evacuate people inside the building immediately.

(A) crack

(B) cracked

(C) compose

(D) composed

10 Why he felt so _____ on Friday is not understandable because he slept all day long that day.

(A) tired

(B) tiring

(C) be tired

(D) being tired

8 The process _____ in the conversion of an oil into margarine is known as hydrogenarion.

(A) involve

(B) involved

(C) involving

(D) can involve

11 Whether Jacob is _____ with learning science is her big concern as she wants him to be a scientist.

(A) pleased

(B) pleasing

(C) pleasure

(D) pleasures

9 She sat in silence _____ her childhood, missing those days she was free from lots of tasks.

(A) remember

(B) remembered

(C) remembering

(D) being remembered

12 I am _____ whether Andy loves Lily because they are so close to each other but have never gone on a date.

(A) confuse

(B) confusion

(C) confusing

(D) confused

Error Recognition

 틀린 문장 고르기

다음 중 문법적으로 <u>틀린</u> 것을 고르세요.

Tyra's favorite band was having a concert. To buy tickets, Tyra had to line up overnight with her friends, **①** started from early evening. Late at night, she got **②** bored in the line since she had to wait for a long time **③** doing nothing. She put a sign with her name on it in her spot. Then, she went to her car to sleep. She thought people would see the sign and easily recognize she came first. Finally, she woke up and returned to the line, but her sign was **④** gone. When she tried to go back to her spot, people got really angry. As a result, Tyra had to go back to the end of the line. Hours later, she got to the ticket window. But by the time she got there, all the tickets were gone. She **⑤** regretted her judgement.

 고쳐쓰기

틀린 문장의 번호를 쓰고 올바르게 고치세요.

 틀린 문장 고르기

다음 중 문법적으로 <u>틀린</u> 것을 고르세요.

Shoppers, although these might seem to be typical, these are not just ordinary wool gloves. See the ❶ amazing lights on the fingertips? These are LED gloves. These LEDs shine bright when you ❷ press the button. You can use it as ordinary gloves, and also you can use it as special gloves whenever you want. Wear them at parties with your friends. Everyone will love the rainbow-❸ coloring lights! ❹ Wear them for safety when you walk in the dark. Drivers will be able to see your bright hands. What is more, no batteries are required, because these gloves are solar-❺ powered ! Don't hesitate to buy!

 고쳐쓰기

틀린 문장의 번호를 쓰고 올바르게 고치세요.

➡ _____

✏️ 배운 내용 스스로 정리해보기

① 수동의 의미

분사와 수식을 받는 명사의 의미상 관계가 수동이면 〔   〕을(를) 쓴다.

예시문장 써보기

➡ _____ (newspaper, copy)

② 완료된 동작의 상태나 성질

분사와 수식을 받는 명사의 의미상 관계가 완료이면 〔   〕을(를) 쓴다.

예시문장 써보기

➡ _____ (steam engine, invent)

③ 과거분사의 용법

분사가 수식을 받는 명사의 의미를 한정시키는 것을 ❶ 〔   〕이라고 하고,

더 자세히 의미를 풀어주는 것을 ❷ 〔   〕이라고 한다.

예시문장 써보기

❶ 한정용법 ➡ _____

❷ 서술용법 ➡ _____

④ 감정동사

감정동사에서 현재·과거분사 구별은 주어가 ❶ 〔   〕인지 ❷ 〔   〕인지가 핵심이다.

예시문장 써보기

❶ 주어가 사람 ➡ _____

❷ 주어가 사물 ➡ _____

UNIT 03

분사구문

생김새	**(접속사) + 분사, 주어 + 동사 ~** ex) **Getting** a driver's license, she bought a new car.
쓰임	**부사절을 분사 형태의 부사구로 간결하게 만들 때** ex) Though <u>he</u> ran fast, <u>he</u> missed the school bus. = **Running** fast, he missed the school bus.
시제와 태	❶ **부사절과 주절이 같은 시제일 때, '동사원형 + -ing'를 사용** ex) **Finishing** my homework, I took online lectures. ❷ **수동형 분사구문에서 being은 생략 가능** ex) <u>(Being)</u> **Born** in Korea, they enjoyed kimchi.

UNIT ③ 분사구문

① 분사구문의 의미와 적용범위

NOTE ✏️

이유	**Feeling** tired, he went to bed early. = <u>As</u> he **felt** tired, he went to bed early. (= since, because) **Having received** no answer from him, I wrote again. = <u>As</u> I **had received** no answer from him, I wrote again. (= since, because)
양보	**Admitting** what you say, I think you are wrong. = <u>Though</u> I **admit** what you say, I think you are wrong. (= although, even if) **Born** of the same parents, they look different. = <u>Though</u> they **were born** of the same parents, they look different. (= although, even if)
시간	**Walking** along the street, I met Julie. = <u>While</u> I **was walking** along the street, I met Julie. (= when) **Having failed** three times, I succeeded at last. = <u>After</u> I **had failed** three times, I succeeded at last.
조건	**Turning** to the left, you will find the box. = <u>If</u> you **turn** to the left, you will find the box.
부대 상황	**동시동작** I was reading a book, my wife **sewing**. = I was reading a book, <u>while</u> my wife **was sewing**. **동시상황** He lay still, <u>(with)</u> his eyes **closed**. **연속동작** The train left at 8, **arriving** at Seoul at 11. = The train left at 8, <u>and</u> it **arrived** at Seoul at 11.

TIP 분사구문의 확장

분사형 명사	the **wounded** the **accused** the **unknown**
분사형 부사	**freezing** cold **shocking** bad
분사형 접속사	**granted** that **granting** that **provided** that **seeing** that
분사형 전치사	**considering** = for **excepting** = except for

② 분사구문의 시제

단순	**Being** poor, he couldn't afford to buy a car. = <u>As</u> he <u>was</u> poor, he couldn't afford to buy a car. Our bus leaves Seoul at 4, **arriving** at Busan at 9. = Our bus leaves Seoul at 4, <u>and</u> <u>will arrive</u> at Busan at 9.
완료	**Not having been read** for a long time, this book is covered with dust. = <u>As</u> this book <u>has not been read</u> for a long time, it is covered with dust. **Having finished** my homework, I met her. = <u>After</u> I <u>had finished</u> my homework, I met her.

NOTE

TIP 분사구문

● 단순 분사구문
동사 + ~ing, S + V
(주절과 시제가 같거나 나중일 때)

● 완료 분사구문
Having + P.P~, S + V
(주절과 시제가 앞설 때)

● 수동형 분사구문에서
being은 생략 가능
(Being) Raised by his grandparents, he wasn't close with his parents.

UNIT 3 분사구문

Exercise

 ## Exercise 1

둘 중 맞는 단어를 골라 문장을 완성하세요.

1 **Raised / Raising** by Keller, she must be smart.

2 Although he **having been / had been** tired last week, he made it.

3 **Read / Reading** a newspaper, Mike knew there would be an election.

4 **Been / Being** rich, they could buy anything they wish.

5 After Billy **has given / had given** a hint, he could find the answer.

 ## Exercise 2

주어진 단어들을 바르게 배열해 문장을 완성하세요.

1 그녀에게 전화한 후, 나는 샤워를 했다

→ _____ .

(I, her, having called, a shower, took)

2 수학을 공부하면서, 학생들은 지쳤다.

→ _____ .

(the students, exhausted, studying, were, math)

3 에어컨을 끄면, 너는 기분이 좀 나아질 것이다.

→ _____ .

(the air conditioner, you, turning off, better, will feel)

 Exercise 3

주어진 단어를 활용하여 빈칸을 채워 문장을 완성하세요.

❶ _____ an intelligent scientist, he invented a time machine. (Be)

❷ Not _____ to sleep, she decided to go for a walk. (want)

❸ Tracy was riding a bicycle, her older sister _____. (swim)

❹ _____ what he thought, I do not agree with him. (understand)

❺ Having _____ their work, the diplomats took some rest. (do)

❻ _____ this train, you'll get to Seoul by 4 p.m. (take)

Sentence Completion

1 As the temperature [____] unpredictably, winter coat sales increased rapidly.

(A) decrease

(B) decreased

(C) decreasen

(D) decreasing

2 [____] the universe, he found the comet and took a picture of it, which made him famous.

(A) Glimpse

(B) Observe

(C) Glimpsing

(D) Observing

3 [____] the fact that he is gone, there was nothing different compared to the past.

(A) Except

(B) Excepted

(C) Excepting

(D) Exceptingly

4 The hen woke up early in the morning at 5 a.m., [____] 3 eggs at 7 a.m.

(A) lied

(B) laid

(C) lying

(D) laying

5 [____] to elderly care facility last week, I visited there twice more in order to give some help.

(A) Be

(B) Will be

(C) Having been

(D) Have been gone

6 [____] the essay, you will be able to check your own performance.

(A) Subsiding

(B) Submitting

(C) Has subsided

(D) Has submitted

7 The _____ were taken to a temporary treatment center.

(A) wound
(B) wounded
(C) wounding
(D) be wounded

8 _____ home after graduation, Dimma had a hard time finding a job.

(A) Left
(B) Leave
(C) Been Left
(D) Having left

9 Not _____ for five years because of other cases, the case was entirely forgotten.

(A) discussing
(B) having discussed
(C) had been discussed
(D) having been discussed

10 _____ lazy, Nick even forgot to do his homework so he couldn't receive a good grade.

(A) Being
(B) Had be
(C) Have be
(D) Having being

11 _____ in space, Yuri Gagarin and Neil Armstrong took one step closer to scientific development.

(A) Flown
(B) Flying
(C) Had flown
(D) Having been flown

12 After Chris _____ the concert tickets, he asked his younger brother to go together.

(A) obtain
(B) obtaining
(C) had obtained
(D) having obtained

UNIT 3 분사구문

Error Recognition

 틀린 문장 고르기

다음 중 문법적으로 <u>틀린</u> 것을 고르세요.

Our city ① **was hit** by an earthquake last weekend. My parents were worried and bought a new emergency kit. It is a 4-person, 3-day emergency kit, but it was a bit expensive. It cost $120. It is large (20 X 40 inches), and it came with a backpack. It ② **includes** a portable emergency radio, 2 water containers, 6 packs of food bars, 1 emergency whistle, masks, and a first-aid kit. Even though these were good items, I still ③ **thought** they were not enough. To make a good kit, we also needed blankets, a hair comb, and shampoo. ④ **Added** these to the emergency kit, I hoped there would be no more ⑤ **risk-inducing** earthquakes. Nevertheless, it feels good to be prepared.

 고쳐쓰기

틀린 문장의 번호를 쓰고 올바르게 고치세요.

⟶ _____

틀린 문장 고르기

다음 중 문법적으로 <u>틀린</u> 것을 고르세요.

The boy now ❶ playing hockey is Milo. His hockey bags are full. He has his own skates and a good hockey stick that was his older sister's. The bottom of the stick is ❷ wrapped in strong black tape. Milo also has shin pads to cover his legs below the knee. He has shoulder pads to protect his chest and shoulders. ❸ Thought those stiff pads make him hard to move, he doesn't like wearing them. His gray elbow pads protect him from falls, which❹ occur frequently during hockey practice. And of course, he has a strong helmet. The helmet has a wire cage in the front to protect the face. Under the cage, Milo wears a mouth guard to protect his teeth. In short, Milo's hockey bags ❺ contain a lot of safety equipment to help him play hockey.

고쳐쓰기

틀린 문장의 번호를 쓰고 올바르게 고치세요.

 배운 내용 스스로 정리해보기

① 분사구문의 의미와 적용범위

분사구문은 ❶ 이유, ❷ 양보, ❸ 시간, ❹ 조건, ❺ 부대상황을 나타내는 부사절 역할을 한다.

주절의 주어와 분사구문의 관계가 능동이면 ❻ ＿＿＿＿＿, 수동이면 ❼ ＿＿＿＿＿ 을(를) 쓴다.

예시문장 써보기

❶ 이유 ➜ ＿＿＿＿＿＿＿＿＿＿＿＿＿＿＿＿＿＿＿＿＿＿＿＿＿＿

❷ 양보 ➜ ＿＿＿＿＿＿＿＿＿＿＿＿＿＿＿＿＿＿＿＿＿＿＿＿＿＿

❸ 시간 ➜ ＿＿＿＿＿＿＿＿＿＿＿＿＿＿＿＿＿＿＿＿＿＿＿＿＿＿

❹ 조건 ➜ ＿＿＿＿＿＿＿＿＿＿＿＿＿＿＿＿＿＿＿＿＿＿＿＿＿＿

❺ 부대상황 ➜ ＿＿＿＿＿＿＿＿＿＿＿＿＿＿＿＿＿＿＿＿＿＿＿＿

② 분사구문의 시제

분사구문에는 ❶ ＿＿＿＿＿ 와 ❷ ＿＿＿＿＿ 가 있는데, ❷ ＿＿＿＿＿ 의 경우 주절의 시제보다

분사구문의 내용이 더 먼저 일어난 경우 ❸ ＿＿＿＿＿ 을(를) 쓴다.

예시문장 써보기

❶ 단순시제 ➜ ＿＿＿＿＿＿＿＿＿＿＿＿＿＿＿＿＿＿＿＿＿＿＿＿＿＿＿

❷ 완료시제 ➜ ＿＿＿＿＿＿＿＿＿＿＿＿＿＿＿＿＿＿＿＿＿＿＿＿＿＿＿

UNIT 04

독립분사구문

생김새	**(접속사) + 주어 + 분사, 주어 + 동사 ~** ex) Rosie getting a driver's license, I was happy.
쓰임	**분사구문의 의미상 주어** ex) If Vella **finishes** a marathon, I will buy new shoes for her. 　= Vella **finishing** a marathon, I will buy new shoes for her. ex) If we **speak** frankly, I love holidays. 　= Frankly **speaking**, I love holidays.

UNIT **4** 독립분사구문

1 분사구문의 특징

1. 접속사 생략: 보통 생략되지만 뜻을 명확히 하기 위해 생략하지 않을 수도 있다.
2. 주어 생략: 주절의 주어와 같은 경우에만 생략 가능하다.
   주절의 주어와 다른 경우 생략하지 않고 의미상 주어로 남는다.
3. 동사의 분사로의 전환: 시제에 유의해 주절의 동사보다 한 시제 앞설 경우
   완료형(having + p.p)으로 쓴다.

> As she felt starving, she ate some bread.
> 접속사 주어 동사   주어(동일) 동사
>
> = ~~As she~~ **Feeling** starving, she ate some bread.
>   분사구문   주어 동사
>
> If you turn to the left, you will find the police station.
> 접속사 주어 동사   주어(동일)   동사
>
> = ~~If you~~ **Turning** to the left, you will find the police station.
>   분사구문   주어   동사

2 분사구문의 의미상 주어 생략

❶ 주절의 주어와 같을 때

> If I had known of your arrival, I would have informed her.
> 접속사 주어 동사   주어(동일)   동사
>
> = ~~If I~~ **Having known** of your arrival, I would have informed her.
>   분사구문   주어   동사

❷ 무인칭 독립분사구문

> If we speak generally, boys are fond of girls.
> 접속사 주어 동사   주어 동사
>
> = ~~If we~~ Generally **speaking**, boys are fond of girls.
>   분사구문   주어 동사
>
> If we speak frankly, your life is different from others.
> 접속사 주어 동사   주어 동사
>
> = ~~If we~~ Frankly **speaking**, your life is different from others.
>   분사구문   주어 동사

❸ 분사구문의 의미상 주어 명시

If <u>weather</u> <u>permits</u>, <u>the party</u> <u>will be held</u>.
접속사　주어　　　　동사　　　　　주어　　　　　동사

= ~~If~~ <u>Weather</u> <u>permitting</u>, <u>the party</u> <u>will be held</u>.
　　　주어　　　분사구문　　　주어　　　　동사

As <u>the sun</u> <u>had set</u>, <u>we</u> <u>gave up</u> looking for them.
접속사　주어　　　동사　　　주어　　동사

= ~~As~~ <u>The sun</u> <u>having set</u>, <u>we</u> <u>gave up</u> looking for them.
　　　주어　　　분사구문　　　주어　　동사

➜ **인칭대명사는 의미상 주어로 쓰지 않는다.**

- (Being) rich, <u>he</u> was envied by them.
≠ <u>He</u> being rich, they envied him. (X)

➜ **it, there, 지시대명사, 사람에 대한 고유명사는 의미상 주어로 쓰인다.**

- <u>It</u> being a fine day, I went on a picnic.
비인칭주어 It

- <u>There</u> (being) nothing to do, I went to the movies.
유도부사 There

- <u>This</u> done, he was allowed to go home.
지시대명사 This

- <u>Jane</u> having left the room, Tom disclosed his secret to me.
고유명사

❹ Being과 Having been의 생략

<u>Being a brave soldier</u>, <u>he</u> <u>was</u> not afraid of anything.
　　분사구문　　　　　주어　동사

= ~~Being~~ <u>A brave soldier</u>, <u>he</u> <u>was</u> not afraid of anything.
　　　　　　　　　　　　주어　동사

<u>School</u> <u>having been</u> over, <u>they</u> <u>went</u> swimming.
주어　　　분사구문　　　　　　주어　　동사

= <u>School</u> ~~having been~~ over, <u>they</u> <u>went</u> swimming.
　주어　　　　　　　　　　　주어　　동사

TIP Being과 Having been

● 동명사에서는 생략되지 않음.

UNIT 4 동명사구문

Exercise

Exercise 1

둘 중 맞는 단어를 골라 문장을 완성하세요.

➊ **Known / Knowing** his grade, James studied even harder.

➋ Frankly **spoken / speaking** I don't trust her.

➌ Having **done / doing** their work, my parents took me to the sea.

➍ My teacher **permitted / permitting** , I will go home earlier today.

➎ Melly **given / giving** the donut, the boy is happy now.

Exercise 2

주어진 분사구문을 원래 문장으로 바꾸세요.

➊ Not knowing her name, he had no choice but to wait for her.

→ _____, he had no choice but to wait for her.

➋ Generally speaking, the smarter you become, the more popular you get.

→ _____, the smarter you become, the more popular you get.

➌ The greatest singer, Jessica was famous all around the world.

→ _____, Jessica was famous all around the world.

 Exercise 3

주어진 문장을 분사구문으로 바꾸세요

---

❶ If I meet her tomorrow, I will let her know this news.

→ _____ .

❷ After the girl read the book, she left the library.

→ _____ .

❸ After the boys finished their homework, they went to the public stadium.

→ _____ .

❹ As Fin was a big fan of Laura, he sent a letter to her.

→ _____ .

❺ If your mom opens the box, you will be surprised.

→ _____ .

❻ If we speak frankly, the most important thing in your life is yourself.

→ _____ .

Sentence Completion

① _____ of the man being released from prison, people trembled for fear.

(A) Know

(B) Known

(C) Had known

(D) Having known

② _____ the unexpected result, the pharmacists were in a hurry to invent new medicines.

(A) Having heard

(B) Having hearing

(C) Having listened

(D) Having listening

③ _____ the baseball game, Austin and Jack were deeply impressed by the players' teamwork.

(A) Having seen

(B) Having seeing

(C) Having watched

(D) Having watching

④ While _____ up the mountain, some rocks broke loose.

(A) climb

(B) climbed

(C) climbing

(D) being climbed

⑤ If we _____, exercising is the best way to lose weight, but it is hard to actually do it regularly.

(A) generally speak

(B) speak generally

(C) generally speaking

(D) speaking generally

⑥ _____, he is not as handsome as he thinks, but he is a very competent person.

(A) Spoke

(B) Spoken

(C) Speaking frankly

(D) Frankly speaking

7 As _____ closed, the children couldn't see the elephant, so they were disappointed.

(A) was

(B) having

(C) the zoo was

(D) the zoo having

10 The rock _____ the truth, people are waiting in a long line to ask their questions.

(A) told

(B) telling

(C) is telling

(D) was telling

8 _____, she had to start working since when she was young in order to live her life.

(A) Poor

(B) Is poor

(C) She is poor

(D) She being poor

11 _____, Lara was able to do a part time job without her parent's approval.

(A) Is 20 years old

(B) Being 20 years old

(C) Having 20 years old

(D) Having being 20 years old

9 _____ the secret wall, Selly decided to find another place to hide the diamond.

(A) Founded

(B) Wendy Found

(C) Being founded

(D) Wendy having found

12 The watch _____, my grandfather was planning to buy a new one.

(A) broken

(B) breaking

(C) is broken

(D) had been broken

Error Recognition

 틀린 문장 고르기

다음 중 문법적으로 <u>틀린</u> 것을 고르세요.

Naomi lived in a small college town. She had recently graduated from the local university and was still ❶ living at home with her parents. Most of the people she socialized with in school had either moved back home after ❷ graduating or had left the town for jobs in the city. She was very bored and wanted to make some friends. However, she was rather shy. She worked as a librarian but did not have many chances to ❸ talk with other people. One day, she joined an online book club. It was a social website where people could leave comments about the books they had read. She got to know Avery, who often left ❹ encouraging comments on Naomi's book reviews. They decided to meet at one of the book club's offline meetings. To their surprise, Avery lived only 20 minutes away from Naomi. Naomi ❺ wanted to meet local friends, they were so happy to find each other.

 고쳐쓰기

틀린 문장의 번호를 쓰고 올바르게 고치세요.

　　　　➡　_____

 틀린 문장 고르기

다음 중 문법적으로 <u>틀린</u> 것을 고르세요.

On her seventh birthday, Lili received a train set. **①** Wanted a train set, she was extremely grateful and happy about it. She and her mom took all of the parts out of the box and put them together. However, right away the train **②** set had a problem. The train went around the track without a hitch the first time. But the second time around, it was too fast on the track and **③** flew off. Lili and her mom took the track apart to see what was the problem. However, when they put it back together, the same problem **④** happened . Even worse, this time, the wheels flew off of the train. In the end, Lili's mom sent the **⑤** broken train set back to the store, and Lili played with her airplane set instead.

 고쳐쓰기

틀린 문장의 번호를 쓰고 올바르게 고치세요.

✏️ 배운 내용 스스로 정리해보기

① 분사구문의 특징

분사구문의 특징으로는 ❶ ＿＿＿＿, ❷ ＿＿＿＿, ❸ ＿＿＿＿ 이(가) 있다.

② 분사구문의 의미상 주어 생략

❶ 주절이 주어와 동일할 때와 ❷ ＿＿＿＿ 일 경우 분사구문의 의미상 주어를 생략할 수 있다.

예시문장 써보기

무인칭 독립분사구문➜ ＿＿＿＿＿＿＿＿＿＿＿＿＿＿＿＿＿＿＿＿＿

③ 분사구문의 의미상 주어 명시

분사구문의 주어가 주절의 주어와 다를 때 분사구문의 의미상 주어를 명시한다.
이때 ❶ ＿＿＿＿ 은(는) 의미상 주어로 쓰이지 않으며, ❷ ＿＿＿＿, ❸ ＿＿＿＿,
❹ 지시대명사, ❺ 사람에 대한 고유명사는 의미상 주어로 쓰인다.

예시문장 써보기

❶ 의미상 주어 It ➜ ＿＿＿＿＿＿＿＿＿＿＿＿＿＿＿＿＿＿＿＿

❷ 의미상 주어 there

➜ ＿＿＿＿＿＿＿＿＿＿＿＿＿＿＿＿＿＿＿＿＿＿＿＿

④ Being과 Having been의 생략

분사구문에서 ❶ ＿＿＿＿ 와(과) ❷ ＿＿＿＿ 은(는) 생략될 수 있다.

예시문장 써보기

❶ Being 생략 ➜ ＿＿＿＿＿＿＿＿＿＿＿＿＿＿＿＿＿＿＿

❷ Having been 생략 ➜ ＿＿＿＿＿＿＿＿＿＿＿＿＿＿＿＿

TOSEL 실전문제 ❸

PART 6. Sentence Completion

DIRECTIONS: In this portion of the test, you will be given 10 incomplete sentences. From the choices provided, choose the word or words that correctly complete the sentence. Then, fill in the corresponding space on your answer sheet.

1. All freshman students are required to attend the orientation session _____ for March 1.

   (A) schedule
   (B) scheduled
   (C) scheduling
   (D) to schedule

2. Anyone _____ to volunteer to help out at the Bluelands Theatre Festival, please fill in this form.

   (A) wish
   (B) wished
   (C) wishes
   (D) wishing

3. Lucas Chaton has starred in several of the most _____ horror films of the past ten years.

   (A) thrill
   (B) thriller
   (C) thrilled
   (D) thrilling

4. Kennedy Art School is granting _____ deadline to those who are experiencing technical difficulties with the online application system.

   (A) extend
   (B) extended
   (C) extensive
   (D) extending

5. Editing the book is the most fun, but also the most _____ part of the process.

   (A) time-consumed
   (B) time-consuming
   (C) consumed-time
   (D) consuming-time

6. _____ to the right and going all the way to the dormitory, you will find the food truck.

   (A) Turned
   (B) Turning
   (C) Had turned
   (D) Being turned

7. _____ in plain English, McCarthy's new novel is easy to understand.

(A) Write
(B) Written
(C) Writing
(D) To write

10. When first _____ , it is important to take enough time to warm up.

(A) swim
(B) swam
(C) swimming
(D) being swum

8. _____ his homework first, Mike helped his sister do her homework.

(A) finished
(B) had finished
(C) being finished
(D) Having finished

11. _____ , I spend two to three hours on the subway or on buses every day, occasionally more.

(A) Speak
(B) Spoke
(C) Speaking roughly
(D) Roughly speaking

9. _____ in the city center, the Gwang Moon Hotel is an ideal choice for seeing the highlights of Seoul.

(A) Locate
(B) Located
(C) Locating
(D) To locate

12. Today _____ a holiday, we have no school and will go for a picnic in the mountains.

(A) is
(B) is on
(C) been
(D) being

TOSEL 실전 문제

Error Recognition

● TOSEL 기출문제 변형 수능/내신 출제유형

 (1~2) 다음 중 문법적으로 틀린 것을 골라 고치세요.

1

I had a ❶ wild time at the hockey game last night. After scoring a goal, the members of one team started ❷ shouting at the other team. They threw their gloves on the ice, and a big fight started. The audience got ❸ exciting and started fighting with each other too. I don't like fights, so I left the hockey arena ❹ early . Maybe next time I'll ❺ go to a ping-pong tournament.

➡ _____

2

If you're **①** think of planting a garden this year, there are a few things you should know. If you plant peas or cucumbers, be sure to cover them with plastic **②** to protect them from birds. Also, if there is a sudden storm, **③** bring your tomatoes inside to prevent damage. Lastly, **④** growing onions from seed takes a long time, so be **⑤** sure to plant them very early.

_____

Error Recognition

3

A coincidence is when things happen in a way that is ❶ surprising . One great example can ❷ be seen in American history. John Adams and Thomas Jefferson, the 2nd and 3rd Presidents of the United States, died ❸ on the same day, only a few hours apart, but in different cities. What is even stranger is ❹ that the day was July 4th, 1826, 50 years to the day after they created the country of America by signing the Declaration of Independence. ❺ Been strange still, the 5th President, James Monroe, also died on July 4th a few years later.

4

A deer stopped ❶ to look at himself in the waters of a lake. "My horns are so beautiful!" He thought, "But my feet are so ❷ small and ugly ." Just then, a lion tried to catch and eat the deer. He ran away very ❸ quickly , but his horns got stuck in a tree and he couldn't flee from the lion. The lion ❹ made a meal out of the deer, his last thought was "I was so ❺ stupid . My ugly feet would have saved me, but my beautiful horns got in the way."

5

Come and have an **❶ amazing** experience at the 4D movie theater. You enjoy most theaters with your eyes, but this theater is a treat for your other senses as well. Our **❷ moved** seats can excite your sense of touch, while your sense of smell **❸ enjoys** our special perfume system. Our **❹ modern** sound system completes the experience. Come feel, smell, hear and see the latest movies **❺ at** the 4D theater!

6

Attention, **❶ valued** customers. For a **❷ limit** time, we are offering a special deal on ladies' boots and gloves. All boots **❸ are** 30% off, and gloves are half price. In addition, our wide selection of **❹ scarves** has been discounted by 25%. This discount does not apply to clearance items. Prepare for winter by **❺ taking** advantage of this special event.

Answers

Short Answers

UNIT 1 p.24

▶ Exercise 1

1. quickly	2. her	3. created	4. at	5. helpful

▶ Exercise 2

1. My dream is to become a world-renowned author.	2. He has firm belief that the economy will recover.	3. Do you have any idea why people are running so fast?

▶ Exercise 3

1. Their	2. well	3. unless	4. Oops	5. within	6. by

▶ Sentence completion p.26

1. (B) notice	2. (A) internet	3. (C) yours	4. (A) swift	5. (B) awful	6. (A) afraid
7. (C) enlarge	8. (A) Prepare	9. (C) more easily	10. (C) bitterly	11. (B) that she	12. (B) even though it

▶ Error Recognition p.28

1. (3) sudden	2. (3) sudden → suddenly
1. (5) headed	2. (5) headed → head

▶ Unit Review p.30

❶ 주어	❷ 목적어	❸ 보어	❹ 수식어	❺ 서술어

❶ I have difficulty in finding the hotel.	❷ He was annoyed by her.	❸ I am exhausted.	❹ My income was increased.	❺ I think today is exceptionally cold.	❻ I need more time to prepare the presentation.
❼ My family planted an apple tree last weekend.	❽ This plan is significant because today is my wedding anniversary.	❾ He accidentally met an old friend of his in the restaurant.			❿ It takes 25 minutes to get to school from here.

UNIT 2 p.34

▶ Exercise 1

1. calls	2. for me	3. that I	4. me	5. us pizza

▶ Exercise 2

1. The school offered a full scholarship to Jack.	2. I'm planning to cook a French dish for my best friend.	3. Could you get something to drink for me?
4. Gary hasn't sent the important email to the professor yet.	5. Ms. jarrett taught how to play the guitar to me.	

▶ Exercise 3

1. her	2. me	3. for	4. to	5. him	6. you

▶ Sentence completion p.36

1. (A) me	2. (B) is	3. (A) found me	4. (B) give	5. (A) showed	6. (C) to
7. (D) for	8. (A) to me	9. (B) find it	10. (A) waiting	11. (A) call	12. (C) him honest

▶ Error Recognition p.38

1. (4) allow for	2. (4) allow for → allow
1. (2) gave to	2. (2) gave to → gave

▶ Unit Review p.40

1. ❶ 주어	❷ 동사	❸ 5

❶ The baby smiles	❷ The student became a teacher.	❸ We wrapped up the project.	❹ Jessica gave me an umbrella.	❺ The school appointed her a school principal.

2. ❶ 4형식	❷ 3형식	❸ 3형식	❹ 전치사
❶ We recommended him the accommodations.		❷ We recommended the accommodations to him.	

3. ❸ make	❶ make / Her competence made her a leading expert.	❷ I insist that a basic human right (should) be respected.

UNIT 3 p.44

▶ Exercise 1

1. during	2. at	3. In	4. in	5. since

▶ Exercise 2

1. There is a hot-tempered tall old woman next door.	2. This situation occurred obviously because of her mistake.	3. The internet is too slow due to server inspction.

▶ Exercise 3

1. Unfortunately	2. In spite of	3. because of	4. definitely	5. because	6. quickly

▶ Sentence completion p.46

1. (C) nice new blue	2. (A) famous German	3. (A) just	4. (B) firmly	5. (B) that	6. (C) whereas
7. (A) for	8. (C) for	9. (C) On	10. (D) rather than	11. (C) Although	12. (B) despite

▶ Error Recognition p.48

1. (5) white tiny	2. (5) white tiny → tiny white
1. (3) quick	2. (3) quick → quickly

▶ Unit Review p.50

1. ❶ 기수	❷ 주관적 평가	❸ 크기/형상	❹ 성질/상태	❺ 신구/연령	❻ 색채
❼ 재료/소속	➡ There are two beautiful large new frames.				

2. ❶ 앞	❷ 뒤	03. ❶ 절	❷ 두	➡ I hope that we reduce the use of plastic.

4. ❶ 숫자	❷ since	❸ from	➡ I've not watched a movie for two months.

5. ❶ 주어 + 동사	❷ 명사구	❶ Although he is old, he doesn't stop studying something.	❷ In spite of his age, he doesn't stop studying something.

UNIT 4 p.54

▶ Exercise 1
| 1. project it is | 2. are the students | 3. did I | 4. he that | 5. ourselves his holiday |

▶ Exercise 2
| 1. Beside Tim is his friend who will transfer to the other school today. | 2. It was not until 1938 that World War II borke out. | 3. The clothes I ordered yesterday were a lot smaller than I expected. |

▶ Exercise 3
| 1. approve | 2. disappointed | 3. died | 4. lies | 5. know | 6. were |

▶ Sentence completion p.56
| 1. (A) is | 2. (D) have | 3. (C) I gained | 4. (B) are | 5. (C) were | 6. (C) was |
| 7. (B) when | 8. (C) whom | 9. (A) itself | 10. (B) himself | 11. (D) much | 12. (B) very |

▶ Error Recognition p.58
| 1. (2) when | 2. (2) when → where[that] |
| 1. (3) very | 2. (3) very → far |

▶ Unit Review p.60
| 1. ❶ 목적어 | ❷ 보어 | ❸ 부사(구) | ❹ 주어 | ❺ 동사 |

➔ Well do I remember the book I read with her.

| 2. ➔ So happy was she that she couldn't sit still. | 3. ➔ It was them that[whom] you saw in the museum. |

| 4. ❶ 명사/대명사 | ➔ He himself couldn't believe the news. |

| 5. ❶ Brian is much taller than his brother. | ❷ Asia is by far the biggest continent. |

TOSEL 실전문제 1
1. (A) length	2. (A) it	3. (B) rental	4. (C) on	5. (C) feet cosy	6. (A) found her
7. (B) considers him	8. (C) three nice big new yellow	9. (C) promptly	10. (B) In spite of	11. (B) Never	12. (A) that
1. (4) especial → especially	2. (4) to ecosysem destruction → ecosystem destruction	3. (2) truly
4. (1) strong extra	5. (3) has	6. (5) he

CHAPTER 2 p.71

UNIT 1 p.72

▶ Exercise 1
| 1. hold | 2. shouting | 3. helps | 4. may | 5. must | 6. have read |

▶ Exercise 2
| 1. The doctor knew her patient suffer an irritable colon syndrome | 2. My brother had better take some rest to relieve stress on weekend. | 3. He might have spent the whole day searching for the materials for assignments. |

▶ Exercise 3
| 1. memorize / memorizing | 2. touching | 3. (to) reduce | 4. sign | 5. study | 6. could have prevented |

▶ Sentence completion p.74
| 1. (A) enter | 2. (A) twinkle | 3. (C) committing | 4. (B) staring | 5. (A) practice | 6. (A) has |
| 7. (A) Let | 8. (A) may invade | 9. (D) would rather | 10. (B) should | 11. (D) should have chosen | 12. (B) must have not repaired |

▶ Error Recognition p.76
| 1. (2) to create | 2. (2) to create → create |
| 1. (5) could have taken | 2. (5) could have taken → must have taken |

▶ Unit Review p.78
| 1. ❶ 원형부정사 | ❷ 능동 | ❸ 동사원형[원형부정사] | ❹ 현재분사(ing) | ❺ 현재분사(ing) |

| ❶ Kimberly hears Hugo play[playing] the guitar. | ❷ Emily had his son pick her up. | ❸ Dennis helped his friend (to) do his homework. |

| 2. ❶ be | ❷ 일반 | ❸ 원형부정사 |

| ❶ You may go home now. | ❷ You must bring the prescription in order to receive your drugs. | ❸ We should have gotten a taxi. |

UNIT 2 p.82

▶ Exercise 1
| 1. To spend | 2. to manage | 3. to study | 4. to drink | 5. to make |

▶ Exercise 2
| 1. To be honest, I want to leave this room right now. | 2. My sister played the violin hard to become a great violinist. | 3. Nina may be sick to miss the class meeting. |

▶ Exercise 3
| 1. to go | 2. be | 3. to apologize | 4. to hear | 5. to receive | 6. disappointed |

▶ Sentence completion p.84
| 1. (D) To speak | 2. (D) To visit | 3. (C) to travel | 4. (B) to do | 5. (C) to come | 6. (B) to prepare |
| 7. (D) in which | 8. (A) to report | 9. (B) to stay | 10. (C) enough | 11. (C) small | 12. (D) would contribute |

▶ Error Recognition p.86
| 1. (3) so attract | 2. (3) so attract → to attract |
| 1. (1) was | 2. (1) was → would |

▶ Unit Review p.88
| 1. ❶ 주어 | ❷ 보어 | ❸ 목적어 |

| ❶ To wake up early is hard for me. | ❷ My dream is to travel America. |

| 2. ❶ 명사 | ❷ 보어 |

| ❶ We need something new to do. | ❷ Ben is to come this party. |

| 3. ❶ 목적 | ❷ 결과 | ❸ 원인 |

| ❶ She came home early to clean her room. | ❷ My daughter grew up to be a beautiful lady. |

UNIT 3 p.92

Exercise 1
1. Drinking　2. working　3. solving　4. utilizing　5. doing

Exercise 2
1. Having diverse experience affects choosing an occupation.
2. What I have to do is rearranging scrambled lists for our projcects.
3. They aren't afraid of carrying out the unprecedented challenges.

Exercise 3
1. collecting　2. working　3. preparing　4. writing　5. investigating　6. drawing

Sentence completion p.94
1. (C) Searching　2. (B) looking　3. (C) living　4. (C) drinking　5. (C) being　6. (C) turning on
7. (D) playing　8. (B) reading　9. (A) is　10. (C) planning　11. (B) voting　12. (C) studying

Error Recognition p.96
1. (5) take charge　2. (5) take charge → taking charge
1. (5) gave　2. (5) gave → giving

Unit Review p.98
1. ❶ 명사　❷ 주어　❸ 목적어　❹ 보어
　❶ Learning Spanish is one of the things on my bucket list.
　❷ He avoided answering my question.
　❸ The most important thing is meeting a good person.
2. ❶ 관사　❷ 소유격　❸ 형용사　❹ 주어　❺ 목적어　❻ 보어
　❶ Here are several examples of the drawing of Geoge Grosz.
　❷ New findings support the existing theory.

UNIT 4 p.102

Exercise 1
1. Rolling　2. for him　3. my friend's　04. winning　5. to understand　6. playing

Exercise 2
1. It was impudent of you to make rude remarks to him.
02. Luca seems to have joined the dance club.
3. The class president is trying to accommodate opposite views.

Exercise 3
1. to get　2. for singers　3. her student's　4. having passed　5. to be　6. editing

Sentence completion p.104
1. (C) to drive　2. (A) solving　3. (B) of him　4. (C) for workers　5. (A) mentioning　6. (D) disappearing
7. (C) to have renovated　8. (D) having applied　9. (B) to use　10. (B) challenging　11. (B) missing　12. (B) baking

Error Recognition p.106
1. (1) going　2. (1) going → to go
1. (2) of opossums　2. (2) of opossums → for opossums

Unit Review p.108
1. ❶ for + 목적격　❷ of + 목적격　❸ 소유격
　❶ It is important for students to ask questions to their teacher.
　❷ It is clever of you to think creatively.
　❸ Wane doesn't like her husband's going fishing.
2. ❶ to + have + 과거분사　❷ having + 과거분사
　❶ They seem to have cried.
　❷ He remembers having practiced the piano every day.
3. ❶ to부정사　❷ 동명사
　❶ He decided to accept her offer after all.
　❷ Do you mind closing the door?

TOSEL 실전문제 2
1. (A) keep　2. (A) swear　3. (B) attracting　4. (C) To build　5. (B) of you　6. (B) difficult
7. (A) may　8. (D) is to choose　9. (C) taking　10. (C) Becoming　11. (B) taking　12. (D) having developed
1. (3) include → to include　2. (1) have get → have gotten　3. (2) of it　4. (5) used
5. (2) to get　6. (1) slowing

CHAPTER 3　　　　　　　　　　　　　　　　　　　　　　　　　　p.119

UNIT 1 p.120

Exercise 1
1. standing　2. fresh-looking　3. playing　4. dancing　5. astonishing

Exercise 2
1. The baby crying is Jenny's younger sister.
2. You are allowed to watch movies containing political issues.
3. They are wearing sparkling clothes which Kim made

Exercise 3
1. singing　2. following　3. sobbing　4. taking　5. remembering　6. solving

Sentence completion p.122
1. (A) including　2. (C) walking　3. (D) looking　4. (D) approaching　5. (D) coughing　6. (A) shouting
7. (C) hibernating　8. (D) wearing　9. (A) leaning　10. (D) fascinating　11. (B) leaving　12. (D) concerning

Error Recognition p.124
1. (3) knowing　2. (3) knowing → knows
1. (2) involving　2. (2) involving → involved

Unit Review p.126
1. ❶ 현재분사　➜ There is an employee distributing flyers.
2. ❶ 현재분사　➜ The man running across the street is my father.
3. ❶ 현재분사　➜ The astronaut wearing a spacesuit is waving his hand to us.
4. ❶ 한정용법　❷ 서술용법
　❶ I'm reading a fascinating novel about a Greek prince.　❷ We saw the ship lying in the harbor.

UNIT 2
Exercise 1 p.130
1. colored　02. open　03. well-motivated　04. gone　05. frightened

▶ Exercise 2	✎	1. When I found her, she was already caught by the police.	2. The students were satisfied with their lunch menu today.	3. Greg is wearing a suit which is made by his father.		
▶ Exercise 3	✎	1. captured	2. singing	3. exposed	4. permed	5. irritated	6. surprising

▶ Sentence completion p.132	✎	1. (D) endangered	2. (C) prepared	3. (C) driven	4. (D) dotted	5. (B) Used	6. (B) increased
		7. (B) cracked	8. (B) invovled	9. (C) remembering	10. (A) tired	11. (A) pleased	12. (D) confused

▶ Error Recognition p.134	✎	1. (A) started	2. (A) started → starting
	✎	1. (3) coloring	2. (3) coloring → colored

▶ Unit Review p.136	✎	1. ❶ 과거분사	➜ She brought a copied newspaper to me.	
	✎	2. ❶ 과거분사	➜ The invented steam engine was an innovation.	
	✎	3. ❶ 한정용법 ❷ 서술용법	❶ A freshly baked muffin is perfect for every occasion.	❷ They seemed disappointed with the news.
	✎	4. ❶ 사람 ❷ 사물	❶ Peter was confused on whether it is a photograph or landscape.	❷ The result was satisfying.

UNIT 3

▶ Exercise 1 p.140	✎	1. Raised	2. had been	3. Reading	4. Being	5. had given
▶ Exercise 2	✎	1. Having called her, I took a shower.	2. Studying math, the students were exhausted.	3. Turning off the air conditioner, you will feel better.		
▶ Exercise 3	✎	1. Being	2. wanting	3. swimming	4. Understanding	5. done	6. Taking

▶ Sentence completion p.142	✎	1. (B) decreased	2. (D) Observing	3. (C) Excepting	4. (D) laying	5. (C) Having been	6. (B) Submitting
		7. (B) wounded	8. (D) Having left	9. (D) having been discussed	10. (A) Being	11. (B) Flying	12. (C) had obtained

▶ Error Recognition p.144	✎	1. (4) Added	2. (4) Added → Adding
	✎	1. (3) Thought	2. (3) Thought → Thinking

▶ Unit Review p.146	✎	1. ❻ 현재분사 ❼ 과거분사		
		❶ Finishing cleaning her room, she felt tired.	❷ Not doing his homework, he watched TV.	❸ Washing her hair, she heard thunder.
		❹ Having much money, I'll donate to charities.	❺ He is drawing a picture, (with) his legs (being) crossed.	
	✎	2. ❶ 단순시제 ❷ 완료시제 ❸ 완료 ❹ having + 과거분사		
		❶ Living in the city, I can easily find amenities.	❷ Having lost his money, he realized his fault.	

UNIT 4

▶ Exercise 1 p.150	✎	1. Knowing	2. speaking	3. done	4. permitting	5. giving
▶ Exercise 2	✎	1. As he did not know her name	2. If we speak generally	3. Being[As she was] the greatest singer		
▶ Exercise 3	✎	1. Meeting her tomorrow, I will let her know this news.	2. Reading the book, the girl left the library.	3. Finishing their homework, the boys went to the public stadium.		
		4. (Being) A big fan of Laura, Fin sent a letter to her.	5.Your mom opening the box, you will be surprised.	6. Frankly speaking, the most important thing in your life is yourself.		

▶ Sentence completion p.152	✎	1. (D) Having known	2. (A) Having heard	3. (C) Having watched	4. (C) climbing	5. (B) speak generally	6. (D) Frankly speaking
		7. (C) the zoo was	8. (A) Poor	9. (D) Wendy having found	10. (B) telling	11. (B) Being 20 years old	12. (A) broken

▶ Error Recognition p.154	✎	1. (5) wanted	2. (5) wanted → wanting
	✎	1. (1) Wanted	2. (1) Wanted → Having wanted

▶ Unit Review p.156	✎	1. ❶ 접속사 생략 ❷ 주어 생략 ❸ 동사의 분사로의 전환	
	✎	2. ❷ 무인칭 독립분사구문	➜ Generally speaking, mathematics is pragmatic.
	✎	3. ❶ 인칭대명사 ❷ it ❸ there	
		❶ It being cloudy, I canceled the appointment.	❷ There (being) something to eat, I didn't go to the market.
	✎	4. ❶ Being ❷ Having veen	
		❶ A competent man, he achieved good results.	❷ The class started, they took their seats.

TOSEL 실전문제 3	✎	1. (B) scheduled	2. (D) wishing	3. (D) thrilling	4. (B) extended	5. (B) time-consuming	6. (B) Turning
		7. (B) Written	8. (D) Having finished	9. (B) Located	10. (C) swimming	11. (D) Roughly speaking	12. (D) being
	✎	1. (3) exciting → excited	2. (1) think → thinking	3. (5) that	4. (4) made		
		5. (2) moved	6. (2) limit				